In My Corner

In My Corner

Reflections on Family, Gardening, Raising Children and Facing Life

Susan O'Brien Fischer

Hackberry Publishing

Cover and Interior Design by Ellen Heitman Walz

Printed in the United States of America

First Printing: August 2011

www.SusanOBrienFischer.com

ISBN 978-0-9837413-0-5

This book
is dedicated to Susan's girls
—Rachel, Claire and Mary—
the true source of joy in her life

The following collected writings are by a wife and mother who shared her thoughts during a very difficult time through web posts, personal letters and articles in The Sedalia Democrat, *the daily newspaper in Sedalia, Missouri.*

1

Grow old along with me! The best is yet to be…

— *Robert Browning*

Brain Disease Mimics Life
January 12, 2006

"Didn't you have any other symptoms during the past few months?" my surgeon asked me the day after my craniotomy, or my "cranie," as the nurses kept referring to it last week.

"Haven't you been forgetting things?" he added.

I rolled my eyes.

"I mean important things," he persisted.

Well, let's see, I thought. I'm 46 years old, with wildly fluctuating hormones and three extremely active children who think my sole purpose in life is to chauffeur them around to all of their various activities.

Some of my dearest and oldest friends, all of them busy mothers, giggled as I recounted the conversation to them later in my hospital room.

I'm essentially micromanaging five busy lives, including important things like doctor and dentist appointments as well as all of the countless mundane things, like vitamin intake, sports practices, water bottles for basketball games, and whether their very favorite shirt in the whole world is clean for the field trip, and on and on and on. Of course, to my children, it's all life and death.

Many days I look at my calendar in disbelief, unsure how I will possibly get my children to three different sport practices, at three different locations, all at the same time. Believe me, the GPS tracking system has nothing on the modern mother when it comes to logistics. So excuse me if I forget a few things now and then. And when that happens, how's a woman to know whether it's perimenopause or a brain tumor? Sometimes it's hard to know which is worse.

So, I do what all other mothers do; I call for help. Thank goodness we're all in the same boat. When a call comes from some other harried mother, we all bend over backward to help each other out.

It's kind of like a club. It's not very exclusive, and there are almost no requirements for membership, simply be stupid enough to allow your children to sign up for every imaginable activity under the sun while assuming personal responsibility for making sure it all happens in perfect synchronicity.

Then screw up and forget where you're supposed to be now and then—bingo, you're in! Obviously, this includes just about every mother alive today.

So, yes, I've had lots of those agonizing moments when I look up and realize I'm supposed to be somewhere else entirely and that it's far too late to actually get to where I'm supposed to be. Just last week I forgot about the eighth-grade graduation meeting at school (er, I mean, I was otherwise engaged and couldn't make it).

I've also forgotten to pay the electric bill and been threatened with termination of service. Luckily, the payment I missed was in July and since the temperature was a searing 100-plus degrees, I think they were afraid we would perish if they unhooked us.

Worse than missed appointments or practices, however, is the mortification of knowing that you've forgotten to pick up or drop off some child, not your own. It's okay to inconvenience your own now and then, but frequently forgetting someone else's child just might get you thrown out of the club. And since we've already established that no mother today can operate from outside the boundaries of the club, that is unacceptable.

So if I've ever left your child behind at a birthday party or forgotten to pick them up on my way to soccer or basketball practice, please forgive me. Because I really need the power of the club now. And I salute all you amazing mothers out there.

But I've got to tell you. Now I have a really good excuse for not being where I'm supposed to be. In fact, I may never be anywhere on time again. Unfortunately, brain cancer isn't a whole lot worse than your normal, everyday life. Go figure!

Six Days Earlier
To: Family Contacts
From: Beth

Susan is out of surgery and resting. Doctors found a malignant tumor but believe they got all of it. Joe is holding up and says Susan is strong and appears to be doing well.

They were able to operate in an area small enough not to require a large area of her head to be shaved.

To: Family Contacts
From: Beth

Susan is feeling much better about her condition today after meeting with her oncologist in Kansas City. The oncologist's message was not gloomy; in fact, she said treatment regimens currently in use are leading to extended survival rates.

Another positive was what the surgeon told the oncologist. Many of these types of tumors, Glioblastoma multiforme (GBM), are sort of star-shaped, making them more difficult to extract completely. But Susan's tumor was encapsulated in a sort of shell, which contained it and made it easier to remove as a whole.

Jan 9, 2006 6:19 pm

Susan is home and thrilled to be in her own house and bed. The oncologist has confirmed the type of cancer. We will meet Wednesday to discuss their recommendations for treatment. Thanks for all your prayers and concerns.

Fischer Family

Jan 12, 2006 9:29 pm

It seems sinful to be luxuriating in such abundance. I have eaten in some amazing restaurants throughout the world, and yet every meal from my friends and neighbors is phenomenal. I will never be able to thank everyone enough. Sedalia is a glorious place to sink roots.

On a lighter note, now that Joe is doing lots of dishes, all of a sudden the leaky faucet is unacceptable! The plumber has already been called. Joe wanted to head out to Lowes to pick out a new one—not. Luckily my sister-in-law was in town so she went and picked out a lovely brushed nickel faucet. Baby steps.

Announcement: Mary is now taking all sympathy orders for Girl Scout cookies. Just because I'm avoiding refined sugar doesn't mean that you all don't need a case (or two) of Do-Si-Dos. It should take at least ten years to really knock you flat!

Love to you all,

Susan

Jan 17, 2006 8:31 pm

Thank you everyone for all of the treatment information. We are looking at everything!

We are overwhelmed and utterly exhausted and still very confused, but a battle plan is beginning to take shape through the fog, thanks to my wonderful, smart siblings and my fantastic husband (my research team).

We continue to eat delicious, wholesome food and I feel as if I am healing already. Thank you to everyone for all the flowers and great meals. We know that every mouthful has been imbued with the healing power of prayer and the positive energy that flows from good people.

Please continue to pray for us for guidance.

Love,

Susan

P.S. To all coaches, scout leaders, etc. I'm sorry we have dropped out of circulation. We have no choice but to focus all our energies here at home for now. We will be back!

Jan 20, 2006 6:55 pm

We are still contemplating all of our treatment options but the head oncologist at Mayo (through a family connection) says that I have a week or two before I have to begin treatment, so that has given us some breathing room. We hope to hear from the Duke oncologist over the weekend and that will help to define our plan even further.

In the meantime I am walking every day, counting my many blessings and kissing my girls whenever they will let me!

Love,

Susan

Charms Comfort in Tough Times
January 26, 2006

Excuse me while I wax lyrical on the magical powers of modern-day mothers. I know men are equally loving and caring, but they are not currently supporting me in a cocoon of creature comforts and optimism.

I have all my talismans surrounding me.

My pashmina from Nepal, sent by a dear friend and mother, who knows that wool, especially when it is mingled with silk, creates twice the warmth to the heart and soul as any synthetic fabric.

My new black pearls, taken off the neck of my younger sister, and placed now around mine. Something I didn't even know about before. As rare and delicate and fragile as my current emotions.

My black velvet cloche, simple and smart, and able even to pass muster with my perpetually embarrassed daughters, passed on by a sister-in-law, one who has survived breast cancer twice, and who knows, intimately, my need to feel human and somewhat stylish during this awful period of my existence.

My French lavender hand soap, which appeared in my hospital bathroom, placed there by my youngest sister, a fairly recent mother who knows instinctively that such luxuries wash away twice the germs and four times the bad thoughts of the typical antibacterial sludge provided by the hospital.

My Willow Tree "Sisters" figurine, one graceful, girlish figure holding her hands out toward her sister, whose hands are cupped lovingly around them. Previously given by me to each of my sisters one Christmas, they are now handed back to me as a reminder of my sisters' love and strength.

The simple gold cross my mother used to wear, symbolic of what was important in her life: faith and family.

Earrings galore, ranging in style from funky and sassy to elegant and sophisticated, some of them from as far away as Israel, Singapore and Italy. Women know that with a partially shaved head, earrings become very important. Men can't even use that ruse to disguise their bald pates! And they certainly can't get away with whimsical hats and scarves like I can.

A tiny origami box with a silver heart inside, made with love by my seven-year-old niece, Helen, who is already learning how to be a mother by spreading her love and concern around in simple yet somehow grandiloquent gestures.

A silver likeness of Ganesh, the Indian deity who removes obstacles and brings new beginnings, taken off the neck of a friend and impulsively placed around my own. "Om Gum Ganapatayei Namaha," my friend said as she slid the silver medallion around my neck where it hangs perfectly over my "heart's center." "May this obstacle be removed, and may I be blessed," she translated for me.

It somehow seemed extremely fitting since I am searching for affirmations galore these days. And though I am Catholic, I have no problem harnessing the energy of a religion that is just as old and mysterious as my own.

My greatest talisman during my illness, however, is all the fabulous home-cooked, healthy meals that continue to arrive at my door every day, with more than a few cups of kindness and compassion stirred in for good measure.

I am well aware of how hectic dinnertime can be around a busy household full of busy children, so I doubly appreciate these many mothers who are preparing two dinners in their busy schedules, one for their own family and another more wholesome and exotic one for my family (judging by how well we've been eating these days).

My husband is getting a good dose of this chaos as well, as he steps, temporarily, into the role of Mr. Mom. He quickly learned that focusing on one task at a time does not work during the busy evening hours at home.

While putting dinner on the table (even a dinner prepared and delivered by someone else) he has learned to perform multiple tasks: helping someone study for a test, emptying the dishwasher, going through book bags, reading and filling out papers to be returned to school, running someone to ball practice before the pot on the stove boils over or the lasagna in the oven gets burned, switching the laundry around from washer to dryer, and perhaps even helping with a few math problems.

During the first few evenings in his new position, I heard quite a few exasperated sighs, but after a while he got the hang of it. It helped that I gave him the secret to success.

"Pour yourself a glass of wine around five o'clock," I suggested. "Just don't drink the whole bottle," I cautioned, because as all good mothers know, bedtime makes dinner time look like a cakewalk.

Jan 26, 2006 9:53 pm

Hello to everyone. We have been tormented over whether or not to try the Duke study of monoclonal antibodies (I know more about that than I ever wanted to!) but have been very worried about having another craniotomy. However, it has been taken out of our hands. Divine intervention, I think.

Last night the head researcher called and said they are temporarily out of antibodies and won't have any more for a month. Since I cannot delay radiation that long, I am no longer eligible for the study. I felt great relief knowing that was not the path we are meant to take. It also would have meant at least two months or more away from my girls.

However, they are working on another vaccine study, which is much less invasive and requires less time away. (Why didn't they tell me about that one in the first place?) But it requires me to delay my radiation by a week, so another agonizing decision. The good news—I can get my radiation here in Sedalia and I've found an excellent naturopath in Kansas City who will work with me to minimize the toxicity of conventional treatment.

I'm also working with a nutritionist, a PhD, who has published numerous articles on battling brain cancer with nutrition and supplements. Luckily, her suggestions are not that far off from what I've been trying to do for years.

But now I'll have to be squeaky clean. No more sugar or refined white flour. Cancer cells gobble that stuff up according to both my nutritionist and naturopath.

I can't express how thankful I am that this part of our journey is almost over. It has been the most exhausting and frustrating two weeks of my life, but I am feeling very well and looking forward to recapturing my kitchen counters and other surfaces from the research papers spread out everywhere.

Thank you to everyone who is buoying me up with love and hope and humor.

Love,

Susan

Friendships Blossom Later
The Previous Fall

"You're my best friend," my 2-year-old niece remarked to her little neighbor, as the two of them meandered their way, hand-in-hand, down the sidewalk toward the neighborhood park.

"Yeah, we don't hit each other," her friend replied, while both of them nodded their heads in complete understanding of this, the most basic precept of friendship.

For my daughters, however, and for all those adolescent girls who recently went back to school only to participate (willingly or unwillingly) in the hallway and lunchroom machinations of their peers, the definition of friendship isn't so easy. That's why, as they wend their way through these turbulent years, I attempt to persuade my own children that for many people, the friendships forged as adults are the strongest and most lasting.

But that's a hard concept to convey to children, when school is all-consuming, and when their circle of potential friends seems severely limited, especially if they are at that particular moment out of the clique.

When I run out of arguments to bolster their (and my) spirits,

I do what I always do when I need good advice. I call a sister. Since I have seven of them, I'm always sure of catching at least one of them at home and she is sure to listen to my ranting and raving, to offer words of consolation and to assure me that my parenting skills are adequate.

In short, she acts as the perfect friend. If someone had told me many years ago as my sister performed a particularly excruciating twisting burn on the skin of my forearm that we would one day be the closest of friends, I would have laughed. But that, in fact, is the truth of our relationship today.

I vaguely remember my best friend from sixth grade and occasionally exchange Christmas cards with my posse from seventh and eighth grade, but my sisters and the women I met in college are the friendships that sustain me these days.

This summer, I spent 24 hours with some of these favorite friends, encamped in a rustic cabin belonging to one woman's family. There, as we talked and nibbled on munchies and sipped wine and discussed all of the important issues in our lives—our marriages, our children, our careers, our "glory days"—it occurred to me that there's a reason my lasting friendships were formed when my need to fit in and to conform was no longer so important.

In college, it was the very differences in all of us that we grew to love and admire. The very fact that we didn't all have on the same tennis shoes was exactly what enthralled us, what pulled us toward each other.

Middle school girls, sadly, are often unable to appreciate that difference, that uniqueness. Too often, individuality is seen as a weakness. I guess that's why middle school can become the "Bermuda Triangle of elementary school," where students "lose their way academically and socially," according to a recent *Time* magazine report.

Many times I overhear parents discussing this very issue. "I don't get involved in all of that," one mother asserts. "I let them figure it out on their own."

The problem with her approach, however, is that the value system of adolescent girls is only partially formed. If we as parents refuse to get involved in social situations (which is exactly how girls bully each other), then we are abandoning responsibility for the moral development of our children, and leaving that crucial area of growth to occur in the vacuous arena of the peer group, where situations eerily resonant of "Lord of the Flies" are likely to crop up.

So, you bet I'm paying attention and getting involved. And as long as they will tolerate it, I will continue to be involved in their social lives and to guide them and counsel them on what I see.

Even if I can't change the outcome of a certain situation, I want them to know how the behavior of others conforms to my sense of morality and truth and goodness. I want them to know that sometimes considering someone else's feelings is more important than doing what they want. And I want them to know that when they do something mean, which happens all too often, I'll be there watching them, too.

But most of all I want them to know, when they're all grown up and on their own, that trying to do the right thing, even though it's sometimes inconvenient and frustrating and complex, will always feel better in the end.

I hope that's a sentiment they'll see mirrored in their real friendships, the ones they'll form when they're finally old enough to know what friendship truly means.

2

Hope is the thing with feathers
That perches in the soul,
And sings the tune without the words,
And never stops at all…

— *Emily Dickinson*

Feb 5, 2006 4:28 pm

We're off to see the wizard! Arrived in Chapel Hill and head to Duke tomorrow morning at 10:00 a.m. Staying in a lovely hotel with a Whole Foods just down the road where we had a delicious organic salad for lunch. Looking forward to a glass of wine with dinner. Joe plans on watching a "little" of the Super Bowl, at least until I turn on "Pride and Prejudice." That Jane Austen always has a happy ending. And listening to Mr. Darcy always makes me feel better!

Love to you all for helping us get here and thanks to everyone watching my girls.

Love,

Susan

Illness Lets Ma Off the Hook
February 16, 2006

Basically, once you get over the panic of having an illness and settle in for the ride, it's actually quite a liberating experience. You get away with all kinds of stuff!

"Sorry, I can't carpool today," I tell my neighbor.

"Oh, no problem," she responds immediately with complete understanding and sympathy. "We'll take care of everything." And I go back to bed.

Initially, right after my surgery, lounging around in bed while my children got themselves ready for school under my husband's watchful eye, just seemed decadent and somewhat sinful. Then one morning I actually did get up.

Big mistake! The mornings I stayed in bed were peaceful and harmonious. Nary a fight nor a scream did I hear, and everyone walked out the door on time after sweetly coming into my room to kiss me goodbye.

But the morning I unexpectedly appeared on the scene again, there was definitely some whining and fussing and fighting from my younger daughters. Obviously, my children need me a whole lot less than I think they do. Needless to say, the next morning I stayed in bed until I heard the door slam and my neighbor's car drive off the premises.

Hours later, still padding around in my pajamas, I felt like a complete slacker, but already my body was feeling better from being allowed to rest. Later that afternoon, I was still in my pajamas, lying on the couch reading one of the many books on my "to do" pile when my daughters barged in from school.

"What are you doing, Mom?" my daughter asked me, incredulous that I was snuggled on the couch at 3:30 in the afternoon, sipping a cup of chai tea. Obviously, sprawling on the couch is normally her territory.

"I'm tired honey. I'm just resting."

"Oh, well, will you make me a snack?" she asked without missing a beat. Okay, so this emancipation theory really doesn't work all that well with kids. But the rest of the world is much more cooperative and sympathetic.

No one calls me anymore to ask if I can attend the PTA meeting or plan the eighth-grade graduation party, or help hand out doughnuts on Student Day, because even though my daughter is the class president, I am off the hook. Hey, I just had surgery!

I don't need to worry about returning Tupperware, or responding to e-mails, or answering phone calls. In fact, I'm getting away with all kinds of otherwise rude behavior because I just had surgery. Now that is definitely a silver lining! I didn't even have to take down my Christmas tree and all the other decorations because my wonderful neighbors did it before I came home from the hospital. I call that a perfectly timed surgery!

I have missed countless basketball games this season, missed my turn in the concession stand, and didn't have to work the clock at the soccer tournament. In addition, my children are disappearing for hours and sometimes even days on end, miraculously making it to all their practices and games, tagging along with friends and neighbors, going out for pizza and attending scouting events.

I do miss them when they're gone, but I also appreciate the quiet when I'm poring over research studies written by neurooncologists. And I especially appreciate not having to attend all of those events.

Another advantage is that really incredible stuff keeps showing up at my house. Even though I am trying to write thank-you cards, I simply cannot keep up with it all. And I have stopped worrying about it, because (you guessed it) I just had surgery!

I like the metaphor used by a well-known psychotherapist who has treated thousands of cancer patients. In his book "Cancer as a Turning Point," Dr. Lawrence LeShan counsels a breast-cancer patient with a story in which a woman is sunbathing.

The woman smiles lovingly at the creatures that come to perch upon her: a chickadee on her ankle, a great orange-and-black butterfly on her knee, a magnificent dragonfly with its iridescent wings on her shoulder, a beautiful goldfinch…perched on her toes.

Then a mosquito flies down, settles on her breast, and bites her. She looks at it and screams, "All right. Everybody off!"

I guess that is what is going on with me right now. I'm taking care of me and fully expect to do the same for many months to come. So, count on me being a slacker for as long as I can get away with it. After all, I did just have surgery!

Feb 17, 2006 6:28 pm

And so it begins. I took my Temodar at 2:00 p.m., then my radiation at 3:00 p.m. My visualization is a gardening metaphor (of course). The Temodar is Roundup (I confess, I have reluctantly used it a time or two in my otherwise organic garden) and I'm spraying it on the pesky white loosestrife, my residual cancer cells, taking over the southeast corner of my patio garden, my brain.

"Be careful of that stuff," my sister-in-law cautioned me when she gave me a cutting of loosestrife. "Some counties have outlawed it as a noxious weed that grows into the sewer lines and everywhere else." I should have listened to her. But then I wouldn't have this great visualization technique.

So after I spray the Roundup (Temodar), I lay black plastic down and then the radiation comes in, pure energy from the sun, straight from heaven, courtesy of my mother, father and sister Margaret, and it wilts and shrivels that nasty loosestrife and my malignant cells as well.

I feel surprisingly well tonight, glad to have the first step over with! Hopefully I'll have some sister time this weekend. Nothing better than a sibling—all that shared history, no need to explain or excuse or elucidate. Are you listening, Rachel, Claire and Mary?

Love,

Susan

Beauty Works From Inside Out
March 2, 2006

Every woman creeping toward the half-century mark, as I am, begins to grapple with the diminution of her earthly beauty. Of course, there are always those women who are even more stunningly beautiful at 50 than at 25, but for most of us it seems to be all downhill with every passing decade.

It gets harder and harder to turn heads, even those of octogenarians. And for a woman who is used to being young, energetic and somewhat attractive, obscurity can be extremely bothersome. The first time you realize your daughter is the one catching the glimpses, it's a real shock to the system!

So even before I shaved my head after brain surgery, I had been dealing with the aging process and the gradual decline in whatever beauty attributes I may have possessed. Easy to say at 30 that getting older will be no problem, but as those crow's feet expand around your eyes and the paunch around your middle begins to widen, exasperation sets in. The young woman who swore she would never even consider plastic surgery cringes at the face of her older reflection in the mirror.

No surprise then, that until recently, an ever-increasing amount of my weekly budget was going toward expensive salon procedures like haircuts, colors and weaves. After all, you have to work with what you have, and I'm not quite ready for Botox yet!

These days, with super short hair I'm off the hook for cuts, and shoe polish would work better on my head than hair dye. Still, I'm religious about keeping my facial hair waxed. Trust me, when you have no hair on your head, you darn sure better not have any on your face!

I always cringe when young girls are so eager to begin shaving their appendages, even before they reach puberty. They have no idea of the amount of time and money they will invest during their lives shaving, waxing and bleaching hair on virtually every part of their bodies. What dimwit decided it was okay for men to be hairy but not women?

Every now and then, during my ongoing "beauty crisis," I rediscover the allure of eye makeup, after forswearing mascara and eyeliner for years. Perhaps wearing eye makeup again will cause the wrinkles around my eyes to be less noticeable, I reason. Putting on (and taking off) mascara is an art form, one that gets increasingly difficult to perfect when you need increasingly stronger reading glasses to even see the details of your face in the mirror. Applying mascara requires a steady hand and a keen sense for detail – not blurred vision.

Luckily my daughter has a magnifying mirror. Ahhhh! Those wrinkles can't really be that bad! And how long have I been walking around with that monobrow? That is exactly why I don't have a magnifying mirror in my own bathroom. Who needs the reminders?

Since my makeup drawer has dwindled in recent years to a little blush and a myriad supply of odd-colored lipsticks that all look terrible on me (free with purchase, in other words), I had to go digging for the serious makeup in my daughter's cache, during my most recent return to wearing makeup. Sure enough, I found every available shade and product line, no doubt all of it from Walgreens, and all of it costing under a few bucks.

As I attempted to hold the eye pencil steady to outline my lashes, I felt something akin to a tremor in my hand. "What are the ingredients in this waxy pencil," I wondered and shuddered, thinking of the all-natural, botanically pure, ecologically harvested according to the earth's meridian cycles, outrageously expensive, imported-from-Germany facial products and makeup I normally use on my own skin.

And now that I'm researching like crazy how to detoxify my body, I'm not real keen on loading it back up with loads of nasty emulsifiers and preservatives usually found in cheap cosmetics. However, my vanity ultimately won out over my repulsion, and I walked out the door in full regalia, probably looking utterly silly, something akin to Cleopatra.

These fears were confirmed when I came back home later to wash it all off and found myself lecturing my own reflection the way I have come to lecture my daughters as they experiment with makeup. "Honey, less is always more when it comes to makeup." Unlike my daughters, however, I actually listened to my own advice and have once again (until next time) given up on camouflaging my aging face with brash makeup. Ultimately it doesn't work anyway.

So instead I'm trying to focus on all the wisdom and experience and mystery surrounding each of those wrinkles and laugh lines on my face. Surely, they are the pure emanation of my unique history and the amazing life I have lived thus far.

Even expensive mascara can't top that!

Mom Goes Rad on Pop Culture
March 16, 2006

I've become a complete embarrassment to my daughters. Situations that never used to bother me seem completely inappropriate now that I'm a mother, and so I find myself complaining all the time.

The first time it happened I could have sworn it was an isolated incident. We were at the movies, out for a family evening of fun and relaxation, and suddenly I found myself in the lobby of the theatre, arguing with the teenage manager over an overt sexual reference in a movie with a "G" rating. Needless to say, my ranting and raving did no good, and the fact that I was nearly apoplectic seemed to be utterly lost on the poor adolescent manager.

By the next incident, I began to see a pattern emerging. We walked into a local video store and there in front of me, tacked on the wall behind the counter was a poster of the movie "Saw." A dirty, dried-out hand and foot were placed at an odd angle to each other, obviously severed from somebody. The title, of course, says it all, so why do they even need these graphic images? I was shocked and repulsed by the display, and bothered even more by the idea that other customers and employees didn't seem to even notice it. Certainly, they didn't seem bothered by the inference of violence the poster implied.

Of course I complained. I can't seem to keep my mouth shut. "That poster is extremely distasteful and inappropriate, especially for children," I sternly admonished the clerk, a pimply faced 16-year-old who looked bewildered, shrugged his shoulders and mumbled that he would "tell the manager."

It took two such visits and two such complaints, but on my third visit, the poster was in fact gone from the wall. I felt a slight thrill of triumph. Perhaps small activist campaigns can indeed yield results.

Many weeks later I walked into a local clothing store for young teens and adults, browsing for birthday gifts for my 14-year-old nephew. As I looked through the T-shirts I read some of the slogans on a few, placed very near the front window.

"Spooning leads to forking," one proclaimed. "My girlfriend doesn't wrestle, but you should see her box," another loudly proclaimed.

Once again, I could not keep my mouth shut! "These T-shirts are very sexually explicit," I remarked to the manager, a very nice, very young lady who smiled, but readily agreed. "What on earth are they doing in a store which markets to young teenagers?" I asked, rather pointlessly, since she shrugged and seemed unable to answer my rhetorical question.

To her credit, however, she did seem concerned and offered to express my frustration to her district manager who was supposed to be visiting the store later that morning. The next time I was in the store, many weeks later, the T-shirts were gone, probably completely sold out to teens (and preteens) who may or may not even have noticed a sexual reference, but thought they were cool nevertheless.

Some stores I won't even walk into anymore. The last time I browsed through Abercrombie & Fitch and noticed the life-size posters of almost nude young women reclining sexily against fully clad young men, I decided enough is enough.

I still wield most of the buying power in my family, and companies that promote that image of sexuality for teens will not see any more of my money. Of course, the fact that the prices are ridiculous, the sizes are skimpy and the clerks are all snobby helped make the decision easier.

My most recent campaign is a personal one, affecting only me. I'm boycotting all of the evening television shows about murder. At the end of my day I enjoy sitting down and mindlessly watching something entertaining and enjoyable. But lately all I can find on television are programs revolving around homicides.

Unfortunately, I've hit a brick wall in that area. I just can't seem to stomach anymore "CSI" and all the other grisly shows determined to outdo each other in portraying increasingly more bizarre, disturbing and gory murders, including disgusting scenes from inside the bodies of the murder victims. Really, life is much too short to be watching a steady stream of such bad news!

And yet, that seems to be about the only thing on these days besides reality shows. So for now I'm filling my evenings with other activities, knowing this is one battle I won't win. But I'm still talking about it to my family, especially my daughters, even though by now they have gotten used to my complaining and are probably tuning me out.

Actually, the more I think about it, I probably learned this lesson from them: if you complain loud enough and long enough, somebody, somewhere is bound to listen—eventually!

Mom Discovers Music Not So Simply Sweet
March 30, 2006

I am probably the worst piano student in the universe, worse even than my daughters, who hated practicing and always crabbed and complained about taking lessons in general. Finally, after arguing with them incessantly over practicing (or not practicing) for months and months, I gave in and allowed them to quit.

After all, I'm the one who really thinks it would be cool to play the piano. I'm the one who feels neglected because with nine siblings there was no time or money for piano lessons when I was a child. I'm the one who thinks that to really be educated and cultured, one should have at least a rudimentary knowledge of a musical instrument.

So why am I wasting my money on kids who have absolutely no appreciation for what I'm attempting to give them?

"Fine, quit if you want to. I'll spend the money on my own lessons," I finally declared.

Boy, have I been humbled. Piano lessons are haaaaaard! Why didn't we all learn musical notes in kindergarten when our brains were like sponges, just sucking up everything around us without effort, hungry for new information, all those brain neurons firing hungrily?

Instead, during my grade-school music classes, we sang songs, memorized words and melodies to recite back during the annual concert. That was a waste of time. And now my 46-year-old brain is attempting to learn a new language, the language of music, and it is excruciating. Nothing I've ever done in my life has made me feel so stupid.

Luckily, as an adult, I'm paying the bills for the piano teacher, so I also call the shots. "Sorry, I hated this song, so I didn't practice it," I tell her one day as we begin our lesson. And what can she say? She certainly can't yell at me. I'm a mom – I do all the yelling in my house!

Unfortunately, I'm worse than my kids about coming up with excuses about why I didn't practice. "Uh, I was out of town this week, a lot!" and "Uh, I really wasn't feeling very good this week."

But my favorite is always the most honest. "You know, this is just getting really hard and I'm not having a lot of fun with these pieces, so we're going to have to go over last week's songs – again."

My piano teacher is very talented and super sweet as well, so she humors me with her kindness and patience, even though I'm sure she berates me as a total loser the minute our lesson is over. Surely, a grown woman should be able to advance at least at the same rate as a second-grader.

Alas, not me! My progress has been excruciatingly slow. Between not practicing and canceling lessons, I seem to forget my old lessons before I even master the new ones.

Of course I don't dare voice my reservations to my children, or the thought that maybe I should quit too, for the same reasons they wanted to quit. What kind of a life lesson would that teach them? That they were right and I was wrong? We don't want any of that kind of nonsense going on at our house.

The whole piano experience would be much better if the piano books were geared for my aging brain. Instead, the lesson plans in the "adult" book I'm using progress quickly with new chords and songs and finger positions in each lesson. Why don't they just slow everything down?

I have no illusions of being a virtuoso at my age. How about a piano book for old fogies who just want to have fun and stimulate some brain cells at the same time. How about providing 10 songs all in middle-C position to be practiced over the course of three weeks, rather than one?

Maybe I should move on to the drums. We have an entire set collecting dust in the basement from yet another aborted music adventure. "You know you can rent these and apply the monthly fee toward the purchase," the store owner advised me when I purchased the shiny blue drum set almost two years ago.

"No, I'll go ahead and buy them now," I insisted, not sure why he kept bringing up the rental option. Duh! We didn't own the set for two months before it became apparent that drums were even harder than piano and, therefore, a lot less likely to be mastered in our slacker household.

Still, I'm not giving up. Perhaps one day I'll play "Wipeout" on those dusty old drums. And won't my daughters be impressed then? As if they really care.

Mom Gets Fill of Field Trip Fun & Culture
April 13, 2006

"We're going to Arrow Rock on a field trip this week," I overhear a mom at school comment to another woman recently. And I breathe a sigh of relief.

Luckily I'm not scheduled to go to Arrow Rock this year. I mean, I love Arrow Rock, but after several trips with grade-school classes, I find myself less and less interested in the movie at the visitor's center and more and more interested in the new latte machine and freshly baked goodies at the general store. I know everything there is to know about the tavern and find myself more fascinated by the gorgeous stand of oriental poppies on the way to the one-room schoolhouse than the real inkwells the kids get to use while there.

In fact, I've become something of a rebel mom on all these field trips. Last year at a music festival in Jefferson City (my third one) I was among a posse of moms who snuck out after our school had sung to hit the new shops on the west edge of town. We had a delightful morning checking out Old Navy, Pier One and Goody's, then met the bus at McDonald's with plenty of time to scarf down french fries and Big Macs. The kids were none the wiser.

I know the right thing to do would have been to stay put and listen to all the children sing, regardless of how long it took or how excruciatingly slow the morning progressed. But after countless field trips, my patience is wearing thin.

I've been to Libby Lu and Build-A-Bear and Worlds of Fun more times than I care to count. I always need to take a Starbucks break before I can watch 20 Brownies dressed up like rock stars shaking their booties to pop tunes and singing at the top of their lungs into fake headset microphones. Call me a party pooper, but that's a sight that requires heavy doses of caffeine in my book.

I've also sat through plenty of math contests and spelling bees and been to miscellaneous other destinations, like the Truman Library, The Children's Literature Festival and Union Station.

But the ultimate field trip was the Mom and Me Girl Scout weekend, spent camping at the Lake of the Ozarks. I had to smuggle in contraband chardonnay in order to get through the entire weekend of crafts and campfire songs. Luckily my sisters were my cabinmates and they were all too happy to partake of the forbidden nectar, so nobody ratted me out.

I know, I know, bad example for my daughters and nieces, unless they learned that when the going gets tough, the tough get going, a philosophy which will stand them in good stead when they accompany their own children on lots, and lots, and lots of field trips! They'll know exactly how to sneak wine into the Girl Scout camp instead of having to figure it out on their own, like I did.

Invariably, the night before a big field trip, once I've finally managed to lay my hands on the informational part of the consent form I absentmindedly signed two weeks before, I realize my child needs a sack lunch for the next day. Of course, it's 10:30 at night, the bus leaves at 7:30 a.m. and I'm out of bread, peanut butter, lunchmeat and any decent snack items.

There's no way I'm running to Wal-Mart at that time of night, so I throw together the worst lunch ever, involving saltine crackers and a bruised orange, hoping my daughter won't check her lunchbox before leaving the house. That way, by the time she realizes what a loser lunch she has, she won't be able to yell at me.

"Who are you going to sit with on the bus?" I ask her as she heads out the door the next morning. Something as simple as this can make or break a field trip. If students get to sit by their friends, they can endure almost any amount of boredom or suffering – even a really bad lunch! But if those friends rebuff them, refusing to make room for them on the bus, the day will be a total failure.

I've watched it firsthand on too many occasions and am delighted that my older two daughters really don't care whether I accompany them on field trips anymore. This jockeying for position on the bus only gets worse during the middle-school years and is altogether too painful to watch, so I'm more than happy to stay home from field trips these days.

Come to think of it, after baring my soul in this way, I may not be invited on any more field trips. And that suits me just fine.

Apr 28, 2006 6:25 pm

Just an update on my latest treatment. After ten days of unexplained fever, I finally started my higher dose of Temodar (one week late) and take my last dose tonight. I have tolerated it pretty well. Woke up with a bad headache one day, but overall the week went pretty smoothly!

I am continuing many alternative treatments and my doctor in St. Louis is very pleased with my progress. My friend Mary from India was here recently to visit. She went with me to my weightlifting class, a far cry from yoga and Pilates, and she walked me through a meditation practice I can do every day.

I can feel a multitude of prayers being said on my behalf and I appreciate them all!

Love,

Susan

Sandlot Games Just a Memory
May 11, 2006

I was extremely grumpy last month when I found myself at the convergence of several sport seasons. Basketball was supposedly just finishing up, yet tournament after tournament kept showing up on the schedule. And most of the teams we were competing against were the same ones we'd played several times throughout the season, or during the many other tournaments in which we had already participated.

Meanwhile, competitive volleyball was still going on, and competitive soccer and recreational softball were just beginning. Didn't sports seasons used to have clearly marked beginning and ending points? Now kids can play one sport almost year round if they want to, and some coaches expect just that.

But not me. I have no illusions about my children getting sports scholarships to college. And I'm not sure I would want them to, even if they were good enough. Having taught at the college level, I've seen firsthand the stress young athletes feel to attend all of their practices and accomplish their schoolwork as well.

Instead, I think college students should focus on their academic curriculum, participate in some college-sponsored clubs or activities, hang out at the local Starbucks discussing Kafka and Nietzsche, and get a part-time job to help defray the costs of their existence. I know sports scholarships can bring in a bunch of money. But there are certain intangibles that accrue from plunging your hands into murky dishwater in the kitchen of the local restaurant, things like humility and gratitude and compassion for those less fortunate.

I've also read that overusing the same set of muscles (by playing only one sport) can lead to serious injuries in young athletes, more so than kids who play multiple sports. And today's practices, especially for junior-high and high-school teams, are much more grueling than workouts from ten or twenty years ago. And they also start way earlier than the seasons used to, only now instead of practice it's called "open gym." Besides, how do you know what you love, and what you're great at, if you don't try everything?

When I was in grade school, I didn't have all of these options. Sports for girls didn't start until junior high school and by that time, most of us were hopelessly inept, having had absolutely no prior training or practice. We were also way too concerned with how we looked and with who was watching each bungled play. Consequently, I dropped out early in the season – every season!

Of course, we didn't have all the modern inducements today's kids do either, traveling to distant cities or even states, eating out at lots of restaurants, staying in hotels, swimming in the indoor pools and roaming the halls until all hours, just like one big pajama party.

When I was growing up that was called a family vacation, and if we were lucky it happened once a year, not during every sport season. In fact, there was no question of ever traveling for a sporting event. Instead, all of our games were played close to home. Even so, I can't remember my parents attending many games, and they certainly never showed up just to hang out during practice. No, my siblings and I either walked or rode our bikes to the neighborhood parks for our practices.

We also didn't have any of the cool paraphernalia that today's young athletes possess: matching bags and warm-up suits, hoodies, scrunchies for ponytails, headbands, wrist bands, sleeve holders, colorful balls and water bottles and the list goes on and on. My kids have certainly benefited immensely from all of the team sports they've played. They're stronger, more disciplined and more self-confident.

I guess one could argue that team sports have taken the place of the neighborhood ball games we all grew up with. Maybe all the neighborhood games have disappeared because we're all burning up the highways to get to our next game – 60 miles away!

For now, we're having fun trying to keep up in the sports rat race. And I'm trying my best to be a good team parent. But we will occasionally miss a practice or two, because, darn it, we're playing it all!

And by the way, it's softball season. Everybody else, off the field!

May 29, 2006 1:55 am

Literally millions of honeysuckle blooms have burst open around our house the last few days and the air is pungent with their sweet smell. As I sat on my patio watching Mary swing, sipping a cup of green tea out of my good china (I'm not saving it anymore), I noticed a mama bird carrying bugs into the hole in our barbecue pit and lifted the lid to see a cozy nest full of tiny baby birds.

My tree roses ordered for Mother's Day arrived and I planted them Thursday evening, and my wisteria from last year has come back and is flourishing. I also had a handyman put up some lattice off my back porch where I hope to plant some morning glories and I pulled the trigger and ordered a patio set.

So, I'm all prepared to enjoy the rest of the lovely spring weather, and we're ready for visitors!

I also survived a Girl Scout field trip to Build-a-Bear and Libby Lu Thursday and school was out Friday.

Trying to live in the moment. And this one is sweet. Going to have a hot bath and read with Mary.

Love,

Susan

Garden Fever Fizzles in Heat
June 1, 2006

Editor's note: Susan Fischer is taking the summer off. She will resume her column in the fall. This column was originally published about this time last year.

All right, I give up! I'll have to wait until next spring to enjoy the pink blossoms of that weeping cherry I have been so desperate for. I'll have to endure another Christmas without decorating my mantel with magnolia leaves, and even though I have already carefully prepared a spot for two dwarf lilacs by my back porch, well, they're simply not going to happen either. I'm out of time and out of money, so my planting season is officially over!

"Planting season?" a non-gardening friend queries. "What do you plant?"

"Everything!" I reply, astonished that someone could be so clueless about the seasons and rhythms of the earth.

Unfortunately, for gardeners, there simply aren't enough daylight hours during the months of April and May, when everything conspires to keep us from our plants: work, field trips, rainy days, frost alerts, hours at the ball fields, empty wallets.

Now that June is here, there is certainly still time to plant, but as we get closer and closer to the dog days of July, it becomes imperative to give new plants at least a little time to adjust before the heat zaps them completely. It's very difficult for new plants to acclimate when the temperature is 100 degrees.

In addition, as summer advances, the selection in the nurseries and greenhouses grows increasingly more desperate-looking, for even professionals have trouble watering pots and flats of bedding plants that are hungry to be planted in the rich earth, so they can sink roots and grow and blossom and flourish.

And then, of course, many of us simply run out of energy. I tried hard to fit it all in. Many evenings in May I abandoned the supper table, replete with dirty dishes, and leftover platters of food, abandoned the book bags filled with end-of-the-year homework, abandoned early baths and bedtimes, or dirty laundry to head out to my garden and work for a quiet hour, trimming, transplanting, mulching, watering, weeding, dreaming.

My youngest kids loved my delinquency, for as I lost myself in my garden, they were free to frolic in the neighborhood, ride scooters or bikes long past the time when they should already have been bathed and tucked in and fast asleep.

"Ten more minutes and you need to get into the shower," I would periodically call out from waist-deep in my perennial bed.

"Okay," they would holler back, all of us knowing full well that ten minutes would turn into an hour or more and that only when the sun set would I finally pull myself from the task at hand to bring everyone inside and begin the nightly ritual of bedtime.

On many nights my back was aching as I crawled into bed, thrilled at being able to transplant 35 rudbeckia plants into the new beds prepared for them on either side of the driveway, or plant three flats of impatiens out by the shed, hoping the deer and bunnies would leave me a few to enjoy over the summer.

On the best of these planting nights a light rain would begin to fall just as I completed my work and I would smile, imagining that healing balm cascading down upon the tender starts, welcoming them to my garden.

Despite all of those hours spent in May, however, I still have lots of gardening to do. Of course it's my own fault. Every year brings more elaborate plans for expanding my garden or redoing a particular area that has ceased to please me. And that ultimately is the great mystery and the great frustration of gardening. The job is never done!

In addition to our own whimsy and fancy, we must constantly wrestle with the vagaries of Mother Nature. Beds that are sunny one year suddenly become shade-covered as the oak tree nearby grows and expands its branches, and I wonder, when did that change occur without my noticing it? By mid-June, the wish lists and plans begun in the late winter, and carefully laid out over the early spring, begin to recede into the cold, hard light of the summer glare.

The first several days in June I watched as the wild honeysuckle blossoms entwining many of the trees and shrubs in the woods surrounding my home broke open, their scent remaining elusive. Then, one evening recently, we came home from the ball field and the air was drenched with the scent of thousands of honeysuckle blooms. The sweet perfume suffused the air, and I knew immediately that my planting season was pretty much over. I'm not sure why, but for me, the honeysuckle is always my signal that I've done enough, that it's time to concentrate on nurturing the plants I've already planted. And to start dreaming about what I'll plant when the weather begins to turn cool.

In the fall, the planting frenzy will begin again, with less vigor than the spring season brings but still with hope and longing for all of those specimens not yet sprouting within the confines of my garden.

I'm never absolutely certain during any planting season what I'll plant, where I'll plant or when I'll plant. I only know that I will plant!

All the details are like the scent of the honeysuckle blossoms. I just wait patiently for them to burst forth.

Oak Inspires Watering Binge
The Previous Summer

The oldest oak on our property was a massive tree requiring two men linked hand-in-hand to circle its girth. Many times throughout the year we would hike the path meandering through the woods, into the back field, to revel in its glory.

It was probably about 150 years old, according to my husband, and I trust him with that knowledge. He reveres every tree on our property, spends hours in the woods examining our diminutive forest, planning which trees to cull so that the others may grow to their full magnificence. His voice is full of reverence whenever he speaks of the "big" oak tree.

These days, however, we view our patriarchal tree with dismay. Lost to the drought a couple of years ago, we finally succumbed to the inevitable, and had the tree cut down. It now lies in pieces on the ground, waiting to be chopped into firewood, or possibly even planed into fine lumber.

For so many years, this giant of a tree sat on the banks of the creek which winds through our property, and used its lengthy roots, even in the driest summer months, to suck up the moisture it needed from the water nearby. But two years ago we watched in frustration as the creek bed dried up, the temperature soared day after day after day into the hundreds, and the tree's branches began to droop. We sat and watched through the steamy days of July and August, helpless, unable to slake the thirst of this ancient tree.

This year, as we enter yet another dry season, after a spring that was disappointingly devoid of rain, I am beginning to see the effects of this latest dry spell on many of the other trees on our property, as well as on our countless shrubs and perennials. But I am determined to save all of these specimens, especially because we were unable to save their granddaddy in the back field. And so, just as the governor is declaring a drought in some of the counties throughout Missouri, I have placed myself on all-out battle alert. My watering campaign has now reached full throttle!

Years ago, thinking myself enormously clever, I installed a nifty sprinkler system in my bountiful flower beds and, usually, by using this system every couple of days we get through the summer with my perennials and annuals still in full bloom. But during these extremely hot, dry days, the dog days of the Missouri summer, my watering fervor reaches a high pitch.

During these times, I feel one of my hoses must be in almost constant use. I have five, two of them with double hose-hookups, making seven possible water outlets at any given time. Because watering during the extreme heat of the late morning and afternoon is pointless, I plan my intense watering regime around the early morning and evening hours, or slow the hose to the merest trickle and allow it to flow into the roots of one of our larger trees overnight.

Many mornings I watch, with intense satisfaction, and an almost meditative calm, as dozens of robins gather in the path of the carefully placed sprinkler heads, preening, drinking and cleaning themselves. Where do they drink when the Earth becomes this dry, I wonder? How do the deer and the bobcats and the owls, all abundant on our property, survive without water in the creek and in the gullies? I assuage my guilt over using so much water on plants that will never feed the hungry with this thought, that the animals are finding solace in the small puddles formed around my dogwood trees, before the water sinks slowly into the earth, sating those thirsty roots.

Some would argue that I am wasting water, even though my home has its own well. And part of me agrees with them. But another, more primal part answers that I am tightly bound to my land, that my obligation is to those beautiful trees, the ones my great-great-grandchildren will gaze up at with awe, the ones that will still be here purifying the air, providing homes for birds and other animals, casting heavenly shade for exuberant children and weary adults, long after I am dead and gone.

Someone once said that because man cannot care for all the Earth, each cares instead for his own little patch of ground. And so I will continue to water my own little patch, and hope that my baby trees will one day reach the grandeur of our ancient oak in the back field.

Perhaps some family many years hence will pause long enough to notice their magnificence, and to wonder about those who planted and tended them, even during the dog days of a Missouri summer.

Jun 24, 2006 10:02 am

Battling a serious illness removes so many obstacles from my daily interactions with people. Consequently, I have had the most poignant and interesting exchanges, sometimes with complete strangers.

My housekeeper, who comes twice monthly, told me that she is trying to take extra special care of me because she knows I have my hands full. Of course, I responded with a sardonic remark, "Whenever you're having a bad day, you can look at me and think, 'hey, it could be a whole lot worse.'"

"Actually," she quickly retorted, "I almost envy you - you have so many people who love you!" Well, I immediately started to cry, because she is right. These two beautiful families, the one I was born with and the one I married into, are caring for me so tenderly and kindly, as are my wonderful friends and neighbors.

Then there was the airport security employee who, seeing me shortly after my surgery on our first visit to Duke, cockily quipped: "Giiiiirrrrl, you just wearin' that so proud!" and she smiled hugely at my bald head and scar, conveying to me more than any other words that all her positive thoughts and kind wishes were focused just on me at that moment. Of course, I started to cry then, too.

Then the last time we went to Duke, we were checking in when the receptionist looked me straight in the eye and said, "You look really beautiful today. Not everyone can wear that look." (Bald?!) Cried again! And thought, wow, this must be a really great shade of lipstick!

We go back to Duke on July 5th and 6th. My amazing sister-in-law is coming with her equally amazing daughter to stay with the girls. I am scheduled to have an MRI done on the 5th. The last one in May showed some "enhancement" which could be bad news or could be inflammation showing the vaccine is working.

I conveyed my concern to my nutritionist who had me repeat a couple of blood tests, and she seemed convinced that my levels are not consistent with someone experiencing tumor regrowth. So that's the story I'm sticking with.

On the 6th I have leukapharesis, a procedure where they harvest my white blood cells to create more vaccine. The last one took six hours, just the length of the A&E "Pride and Prejudice" rendition. Hope my nurses like Colin Firth—I mean—Mr. Darcy, as much as I do!

I am feeling strong and happy and very much in control of this process. Drove around all afternoon in a convertible arranged by a friend at the Chrysler dealer, while my car was serviced, listening full throttle to "Wicked." Ain't it great to be POP–YOU–LAR? My first stop was for a "medical appointment," a euphemism for my weekly massage with my massage therapist, Roy!

Love to all,

Susan

Jul 9, 2006 4:58 am

We are back from Duke with good news and some not-so good news. The good news is they are "calling" my recent MRI stable, which means I am still in the Duke study. My leukapharesis procedure also went better than last time and logistically, everything went off without a hitch.

The not-so-good news is that there is something showing up on the MRI which concerns the docs enough for them to order another MRI in four weeks as opposed to eight. Could be a variety of things, and we plan to find out more when we go at the end of July. We didn't expect to get to see the doctor and the MRI this time, so we weren't prepared with our questions.

Meanwhile, I started my second round of chemo last night. Felt well today and worked in the garden with Joe, but decided not to push my luck by attending my nephew's engagement party in Kansas City tonight (sorry everyone).

When I was lamenting the fact that even being on chemo didn't protect you from being lambasted for missing a family gathering, one brother-in-law quickly retorted, "Hell, if it were that easy, I'd be doing it!"

We ate a fabulous dinner at Nana's Restaurant in Durham while we were gone. I got more than a little buzzed when I decided to mix one glass of really great merlot with the Atavan I had taken to calm me before the MRI. I haven't been that tipsy since I was drinking Rusty Nails at Mizzou! It's a whole lot more fun when you're 19 or 20!

Claire had a great birthday—thanks for all the wonderful gifts and phone calls.

We're taking Mary's friends to the lake Wednesday for a belated birthday party for her. She's pumped!

Love to everyone,

Susan

A Gas Guzzler Confesses
The Previous Summer

I have a confession to make. Even when gasoline costs more than $2 per gallon, I use it frivolously and irresponsibly!

On a recent weekend this spring, I traveled with other parents to Kentucky, six hours each way, to watch my daughter play three games of soccer, during which her team got its collective and proverbial butt kicked. That same weekend, my husband traveled to St. Louis for a reunion with many of our college friends, then drove home on Sunday, and turned around and headed to Cole Camp for a golf tournament. Earlier that week, I drove up to Kansas City, by myself, in a van that seats seven, to do a little shopping and visit a niece.

Just a typical week in our household. Unfortunately, I'm not alone in my habit of squandering fossil fuels whenever possible. Most Americans are in the same boat, which explains why we use 25 percent of the world's oil production.

So I was delighted to hear that the energy policy recently hammered out in the Senate will "reward conservation" (whatever that means). By the time the House and Senate agree on a final bill, who knows what the details will be? Still I'm happy that the word "conservation," at least for now, is on the table.

Because even though I'm frustrated at rising gas prices, I also feel tremendously guilty that I continue to use so much fuel. But I just can't seem to jump off the roller coaster of consumption by myself. Driving these days just seems like what we do.

Surely, when the national highway system began in the mid-1950s, Dwight Eisenhower could not have envisioned a time when parents would use those highways to drive their children an hour or more to take a 30-minute music lesson, practice for a sports team, or host a party for a gaggle of 5-year-old girls at Libby Lu's.

During the '50s and '60s, when much of the interstate highway network was being built, many families had only one vehicle. While dads were out working, moms and kids hung out in the neighborhood or walked to the local pool or park. Kids rode their bikes to ball practice and many parents never even attended games. This was certainly true of my own childhood.

"I paid $2.09 for gas today," my husband grumbles when he sits down at the dinner table after work.

"Yeah, that's too bad, honey. By the way, I need to drive one of the girls to a camp in Mexico, Missouri, this week and then I'll probably drive to St. Louis to pick up my nieces who are coming to visit," I respond.

Politicians have plenty of suggestions for shaping an energy policy, like exploiting the Alaskan wildlife refuge or extending daylight savings time by two months each year. And I guess I can grow used to having a couple of extra hours of daylight during November, but it seems to me we should all work on simply driving less, especially since many experts agree: the Earth's oil is a finite resource; therefore, at some point, we will run out.

Recently I dropped two nieces off at the Amtrak station to catch the train to St. Louis after a visit to their country cousins. I was surprised and pleased at the number of people lined up to catch the train that day: a family of four with bikes in tow, obviously riding the Katy trail; grandparents bidding farewell to sons or daughters and grandchildren; college-age teens heading off to new adventures. The buzz of conversation and laughter around the station was exciting and electric. And the train was only eight minutes late.

On other occasions, I have waited frantically, impatiently, for the train, which arrived 45 minutes to an hour late, even though the information line said that the train was on time. Still, despite Amtrak's many faults, we need to be investing more in mass-transit systems, not less.

I know we're not going to stop traveling, so we need to find easier, more cost-efficient ways to move people around, not only in large, metropolitan areas, but also in Middle America where we deserve choices besides driving our gas-guzzling vehicles every which way, even if our reasons often are downright silly and frivolous.

Perhaps those higher gas prices will finally make me stop driving so much. Unless, of course, there's something really important going on, like the year-end clearance sale at Old Navy in Lee's Summit. Now that's worth driving an hour for!

Jul 26, 2006 10:38 am

We're in Branson for the weekend, living in luxury at the Chateau, eating all our meals out and swimming in between. Then we head to Duke for four days of treatment for me. This time they tag my vaccine with a radioactive molecule and then take pictures of it to try and figure out where it's traveling in my body. This is all done in the department of nuclear medicine, which sounds pretty freaky to me!

I finished my second round of chemo last week and tolerated it pretty well. Luckily some of the more toxic chemo agents don't penetrate the blood-brain barrier, which is also why my particular tumor is so nasty! So the one they've found that does penetrate happens to be less toxic than some of the others.

I always thought I would not submit to chemotherapy if I got cancer, but when push comes to shove, I was afraid not to. But I'm glad I'm not completely poisoning myself, especially since all my other treatment modalities center around bolstering my immune system.

Anyway, I felt much better this go around.

Love,

Susan

Jul 28, 2006 10:38 am

We're here at Duke, had my shots and my first round of pictures. More information from the doctor, too. He explained that the inclusion of this higher dose of Temodar is not necessarily just to kill off the cancer cells, but also to kill off the cloaking device emitted by the tumor to fool the immune system into leaving it alone. In previous studies the better the vaccine worked, the stronger the cloaking device became as well. So, by hitting it with the Temodar, they hope to immobilize it long enough for the vaccine to attack the tumor successfully. Makes perfect sense to me!

Tomorrow we head to Myrtle Beach to have dinner with friends, then to Charleston for one night and then to the beach house on Saturday afternoon.

Joe took the girls shopping for school supplies yesterday (thank goodness I didn't have to do it)! We're having fun road-tripping, not yelling and screaming too much. Saw the Biltmore Mansion on Monday; it was fabulous. Taking the girls shopping now. ("Ughhhhh!")

Love,

Susan

Teachers Can't Fix Everything
The Previous Year

My first (and last) day as a substitute teacher happened quite by accident. I didn't do it because I have an aptitude for it (I don't), or because I enjoy it (I don't). I did it simply because I was in the wrong place at the wrong time.

In other words, I did it as a favor to a wonderful second-grade teacher who has now taught all three of my children, and who prefers to have substitute teachers who are familiar with her teaching style.

When visitors first enter her classroom, no doubt they are struck by the desk piled high with papers and the books that line every nook and cranny of the room, for this teacher is an expert in reading and a great lover of literature as well, and she tries passionately, and successfully, to impart that love to her students.

Like many other talented teachers, her personal motto has always been "leave no child behind" and so she pours all of her energy into her students, helping each one overcome difficulties, nudging them, encouraging them, sometimes even scolding them until they can complete their assignments. The task is nearly impossible when you have 20 students with skills ranging from struggling with vowel sounds to reading two grades above level. It is simply exhausting.

I knew all of this instinctively from helping in the classroom weekly, but after a day of subbing I felt it in every fiber of my body. The day was a series of endless distractions and frustrations, beginning with our daily math equation, which consisted of giving every student an opportunity to figure out how to achieve the sum of 150 (the number of days in school thus far). Invariably each student wanted to begin with 10 and then add 5, plus 5, plus 5, plus 5 again. Twenty times we performed similar mathematical equations. God bless the young man who quickly blurted out 75 plus 75. Simple pleasures truly are the best.

The day continued with a series of "he said," "she said," "he said," "she said." These outbursts were punctuated by the more fastidious students who become utterly indignant at any slight change in the regular schedule. "We don't do that now." "We're not on that page." "The quiet person gets to pass out the paper."

Then there were the kids who can control their bladder during an entire three-hour neighborhood kick ball game, but suddenly, during spelling, have to go to the bathroom immediately – or else!

After the fifth time one particular student asked me to go I gazed intently into his face, taking the measure of the man, or the boy, as the case happened to be. Since the first four times he asked he probably just wanted a break from math, he probably really did need to go this time, but should I reward his previous disingenuous behavior by letting him go again? What kind of a mean teacher would I be if I refused his request and he did indeed have an accident?

By the end of lunch, however, all such compassionate reasoning was gone. I was already crabby, longing for coffee and it was only 11:30 a.m. At recess I was tempted to give all of us a longer respite outside, until I realized that my only break of the day occurred right after recess at 12:02. Needless to say, at 12:01 I fiercely blew that whistle. "Line up everybody!" I shrieked. I simply could not afford to miss that break.

"Man, she's mean," I heard one little girl mutter as we filed back inside.

"Honey, you have no idea," I muttered under my breath.

While I'm somewhat exaggerating the frustration felt during my first (and last) subbing experience, some truths I did glean from my combat duty. In the debate over public education, we are simply asking our teachers to do too much. They cannot, no matter how brilliant or impassioned or creative, make up for what doesn't happen at home.

If children grow up without books and without seeing those they love enjoying books, then they probably will not be readers. And since reading is the foundation of all other subjects, those poor readers are doomed to struggle in almost all other subjects, too.

If children grow up in homes where the television is on constantly and where ideas and current events are never spoken of, then these children will not learn to think and discuss and solve problems.

If children grow up in homes where parents are profane and aggressive in their behavior toward others, or take liberties with honesty and morality, then those children will mirror that behavior, not only in the classroom and on the playground, but probably also as adults.

In short, even a great teacher cannot overcome the deficits of home. But for a child who does have a stimulating home environment, an occasional poor teacher will not hold them back. That's why our second-grade teacher's messy desk doesn't bother me. I know she's working on the hard stuff. She's trying to make up for whatever is missing at home in the lives and minds of 20 students, and while she is very, very good at what she does, not even she is that good.

For when parents abdicate responsibility as a child's first and very best teachers, no one on Earth will have the skill to bail them out.

Spellers Have Nerves of Steel
The Previous Year

The first printed use of the phrase "spelling bee" in America occurred in 1875, according to the folks who put on the Scripps National Spelling Bee. And I'm quite certain, after sitting through a few of these harrowing experiences locally, that today's contests have changed little over the course of a hundred years. They are another archaic remnant of an educational system gone by. They must be! Why else would they be so torturous for parents and students alike?

The pleasure at hearing that your child has been chosen to compete is quickly replaced with trepidation that he or she will not possibly be prepared since the hundreds of words on the recommended practice list simply cannot be drilled before the contest. Add to that the fact that the words can be drawn from literally any of the hundreds of thousands of words out there and your trepidation begins to turn into annoyance.

My advice to my daughters is, therefore, pragmatic. "Just pick up a book and read," which is what they would rather be doing anyway. After all, the reason they are good spellers is because they are avid readers.

Still, on the day of the contest, I torment myself with the idea that I should have drilled them more (or at all) and that I am a woefully inadequate mother because I failed to help them prepare for the torture ahead. But alas, too late now for regrets; the spelling bee begins.

The silence is deafening. The gym doors are closed and occasionally a passerby peeks in through the door window to glimpse what all the fuss is about. But the rule is absolute. No one may leave or enter during the spelling bee, unless there is an emergency. Cell phones and pagers are off.

The contestants squirm and fidget, but not nearly as nervously as the stands full of parents and relatives. Unlike more civilized math contests, where students are allowed to perform brilliantly or abysmally in total anonymity, spelling bee contestants are put on display like prized calves at the state fair.

Willing them to do well with every fiber of their bodies, parents strain in their seats, longing for the agony to be over with, and vowing to work harder on math skills next time. After all, those math parents are simply killing time, visiting in the hallway, even venturing down the block for a cup of coffee, waiting leisurely for their child to finish the test. If their child performs well, they'll receive a trophy or medal, but if their child flubs up, no one will ever know.

In my naiveté during my daughter's first spelling bee, I silently prayed that she would win a medal. Today, after three or four such events under my belt, I simply plead that she won't embarrass herself or misspell her first word, for I have learned that the top medal doesn't always go to the top speller. Rather, it frequently goes to the one with nerves of steel.

I breathe a sigh of relief; my daughter has made it through the first couple of rounds and now, if she misspells a word and has to join me on the bleachers, she can still hold her head up high and know that she tried her best.

I recognize the next girl up immediately and hold my breath. A few years back the unthinkable happened to this poor girl. "Honey," the moderator called out during that earlier contest. "Winnie the Pooh loves honey," she added to clarify the pronunciation and the meaning. The word was easy for this grade level since this was only the first round, but the girl froze from nervousness.

"H-U-N-Y," she blurted out. Even before she finished spelling it, her face crumpled as she realized the enormity of her mistake. Dissolving into tears, certain that the world had come to an end, she left the microphone humiliated, or so she thought.

But I know that every parent in that room knew, without a doubt, that this could easily have been their own son or daughter. Unlike the situation at sporting events, the empathy between opposing spelling-bee parents is palpable.

Today, however, the stars are aligned for this particular little girl. She stands up at the microphone round after round, seemingly cool, calm and collected, even though her heart is pounding, her palms sweating and her pulse racing, and she spells her little heart out. Every word she's ever read comes back to her with clarity and recall. At the end of the day, she is the last one standing at the podium.

Now that girl truly is a winner, I think, not because she finally won first place in a spelling contest, but because she continued to compete year after year, even after misspelling "huny" on her first round.

Aug 24, 2006 11:30 am

I am back from a mountain retreat full of fresh vigor and very conscious of a divine presence in my life. What else do you get when you combine 80 sassy women with no time to waste, no patience for formalities, and no tolerance for ****?!

I also made great writing connections. My yoga teacher all week was the editor of Alternative Medicine magazine and encouraged me to send her my clips, and one of my meditation teachers has a connection at Oprah's magazine and said she would send on an article about the retreat if I wrote it. Well, of course, that ruined any hope I had of actually learning to meditate, since every time I closed my eyes I was writing and brainstorming!

On the final night we had a celebration and participants were encouraged to make an offering to the group. The following piece, titled "Courageous Women," is what I wrote and "offered," in an attempt to preserve what our collective experience had been.

Courageous Women
August 2006

Even stripped down to our very marrow, shorn of our hair, our breasts, our appetites and, in some cases, our very vigor, still we reign supreme!

"Regal as queens," our gorgeous yoga diva reminds us daily and her words become our mantra, at least for these few days.

"I love lipstick now," comments Jenny, the stunning British redhead sitting beside me one morning, and I smile, satisfied with my own perfect shade of Sante Fe red.

"I need a hug," Maria says as we meet in the hallway after a particularly emotional session, and we silently embrace, holding each other tightly, long past the comfort level of strangers.

"My children are my religion," moans Debra as she breaks down into tears, and every woman in the room shudders and offers up a silent prayer for her longevity.

"Don't say you're fine," says Blake. "Fine means ****** up, insecure, neurotic and emotional!"

"Bingo!" we all respond.

"I am Ganesh," Pat bellows in the midst of an impromptu dance session as she hoists Joan on her back and prances around the room, rocking out to the sounds of "Under Pressure!"

Immediately upon taking off her "silent" tag, Amy announces, "I'm definitely going to paint my nails red when I get home," echoing the words of our spiritual dance teacher, that the hands are the window to the heart.

"I guess dying is one of those things you only get one shot at," muses Louise during our break-out session on the subject.

"Welllll, not really," retorts Eileen, a staunch Buddhist convert.

"Some of my friends think I'm dying tomorrow," Molly chimes in. "But, you know, I really don't think I'm going to give them the satisfaction," she adds in her typical Molly fashion.

"Sometimes I repeat myself one, two, three times," Rinpoche, our Tibetan meditation master, humbly admits. But we don't care. We hang on his every word, feeling peace merely through his presence in the room, despite the fact that many of us felt as if we had been thrown into advanced trigonometry before mastering addition and subtraction!

And then we have Acharya Lief, who I always think of, perhaps inappropriately, as simply Judy. She seems the quintessential "sacred feminine," teaching us with kindness, self-deprecating humor and wisdom. And who would ever have guessed, as she admitted to a small break-out group last night, that somewhere in her lineage, there just might be a Bonnie-and-Clyde-type team of vigilantes?

The fact that Jeremy, not Dr. Geffen, but Jeremy, is the only oncologist I've met in my eight-month ordeal that I feel completely comfortable addressing by his first name speaks volumes about his humanity and the fact that he's probably been around for a few lifetimes before this. However, he did seem a little overly enthusiastic when Therese announced that her first goal for the coming year was to have "long and luscious sex" every day! (Perhaps a break-out session is needed on that topic?)

Our cancer, whether we view it as gift or a curse, has catapulted us into friendships that usually occur only slowly, over many weeks and months.

Stripped down by our disease, we search for only that which is true and real and good. These past days we have found all of those things within each other, and, more importantly, within ourselves.

As Linda would say, "Right on!"

Oct 10, 2006 10:15 am

We are at the Durham airport waiting to board our return flight to St. Louis.

We are happy that my latest MRI scan is stable, showing no progression of disease, and pleased as well that the lead researcher agrees that stopping the Temodar after six months is fine and that I can continue to receive the vaccine. That means

I'll take my last round of chemo the week after Thanksgiving and be free of the nasty stuff for Christmas.

Content with our good news and the lattes we purchased at Whole Foods before heading to the airport, we are killing time, anxious to get back to our sleepy town of Sedalia and meet our girls at the exciting "Activity Game" for our school's soccer team.

It should be a gorgeous evening with a full moon and cool temperatures. We'll know everyone there and they will all be solicitous of how I am doing and how our recent trip went.

Some of them will have been on duty during our absence, ferrying my daughters to and fro, attending to chores on the home front, while Joe and I waited (endlessly) to visit with docs and nurse practitioners and administrators and phlebotomists, with a few great meals and a quick trip to Ann Taylor and Loehmann's tucked in between.

The local lumber company will be providing concessions free of charge as a contribution to the booster club, and kids of all ages will be running amok dressed in outrageous costumes coordinated in school colors of red and white, including face paint and sticky hair spray.

They will run around on the fringes of the main event, starting their own soccer or football games, playing tag, or, if they happen to be in middle school, flirting with their classmates, worried about how they look or about their hairstyles along with all the other inane neuroses of adolescent students (and people in general).

But all of these stray fans will gather for the halftime show to watch the "activity queen" being crowned and to speculate about who it will be and who will escort her to receive her crown.

I was glad to hear that this particular queen contest is decided not by a popularity vote. Rather, the crown goes to the chosen representative from whatever high school class sells the most activity passes to school sporting events, proof that as a civilized society, we are making some progress!

After the game we'll round up our brood and pull them reluctantly toward the car, attempting to ignore their pleas to have "so and so" spend the night, and their "promises" to go to bed at a decent hour if we acquiesce.

Regardless of how many extras we pick up along the way home, still we will sleep in our own bed with our own pillows tonight. We will wake up and make pancakes and enjoy our Saturday, in our beautiful home, in our amazing community, and count the multitude of blessings that fill each and every day.

Love,

Susan

P.S. I will not be eating the pancakes!

3

Home is where your story begins.

– Unknown

Learning to Enjoy Silence
October 22, 2006

Editor's note: Susan Fischer is back. After a hiatus of some months, she is resuming her column. It will appear in this space each Sunday.

Ahhhh. Blissful silence reigns in the house these days and settles over me like a luxurious garment. I can hear the birds chirping, the wind blowing through the leaves on the trees, a horse whinnying in the distant field. Thank goodness school is back in session!

I loved having my children home during the summer months when they were younger. We would swim at the city pool, visit Grandma's cabin at the lake, take family road trips to St. Louis or Kansas City to visit relatives, and spend hours outside on the swing, filling the $3 plastic wading pool with cold water from the hose, or catching lightning bugs in the twilight.

As my children have grown up, however, those sweet moments are long gone. These days my summer is spent doing primarily one thing: driving! This nightmare crept up on me slowly over the years, while I basked in the motherly feeling of helping my children be involved. Because I never got to do any extracurricular activities when I was young (ten children in the house didn't allow time or money for that kind of thing), I was anxious from the beginning to allow my children (and, vicariously, myself) to participate in all kinds of events.

It began innocently enough with a ballet class for my adorable 5-year-old. I huddled in the small waiting room with all the other mothers, looking through magazines or engaging in small talk. When her interest in dance (and mine) waned, we moved on. Next came the very first art camp, Blue Sky, which happened to be at the Girl Scout property just down the road from our house. Easy enough, I thought. My girls even rode their bikes to and from that first summer.

Then as the years flew by, more and more and more sporting activities and camps were added to the load, until, finally, this summer I hit the proverbial brick wall. I have grown utterly weary of the incessant driving. My irritation was exacerbated by the high cost of gasoline this past summer, but was really fueled simply by the sheer number of hours I spend mind-numbingly ferrying children to and fro, hither and yon, with more mind-numbing hours on the phone talking to other moms trying to coordinate all these comings and goings.

I could count on one hand the number of days this summer where absolutely nothing was marked on the calendar. "You're running on overload," one of my physicians remarked recently.

"Duh," I wanted to respond, but stopped myself. In addition to driving my kids all over creation these past few months, I have also been trying to search out the best treatment for my cancer and sometimes running all over the state and even the region to accomplish that.

During one particularly grueling week, I shipped in a niece to run carpool for me. She's a model high school student: smart, compassionate, involved—so all my usual worries went out the window. But frankly, I don't think I would have cared what she was doing, talking on her cell phone, driving slightly over the speed limit, applying mascara, smoking a Marlboro, as long as I didn't have to drive for a few hours!

While we were on vacation the first week of August we missed the soccer sign ups. My youngest daughter was fine with that. But I began trying to talk her into playing. "I can still probably get you signed up," I mentioned. And then I thought: What on earth am I doing? I quickly changed tack. "That's fine, honey. We'll just sit this season out." And so we have.

Strangely enough, the world hasn't come to an end. She hasn't been bored, choosing instead to play with her many toys in the family room downstairs or ride her bike around the circle drive. Of course, the schedules of my eldest two daughters are still keeping me hopping, and I still drive a lot when school lets out at 3 o'clock. But during the day I'm purposely driving much less, choosing instead to sit at my computer and write.

Most days the silence is deafening; just how I like it.

Oct 23, 2006 11:41 am

Woke up this morning to a glorious, sunshiney day—just the kind we needed last Saturday when about twenty of my family members were at my house watching the rain, rain, rain. Still, even though the hayride never developed, we had a great time laughing, arguing, eating and cheering on the Cardinals for the opening game of the World Series. Probably the only one I'll watch!

To all my siblings—I loved having you here, but also loved seeing you pull out of the driveway! I appreciate all of you shopping for, preparing and cleaning up after all the meals. What abundance to have so many amazing siblings. We are all by turn bossy, irascible, combative, wise, sentimental, kind, funny and often, just plain weird, a perfect combination.

I feel well today after my third dose of chemotherapy. Skipped my 8:15 a.m. yoga class but made my 9:00 a.m. body pump class. Now I need to focus on finding the perfect black color for a long desk I'm having repainted. As you can see, my priorities are in perfect order.

Everywhere I look outside I see spectacular fall colors, proof of the innate beauty and goodness of the world and its people.

Love,

Susan

Poem written to family
The Previous Year

10

"Ten?" I wonder through all my adult days,
and there have been many of them
"Why on earth did they have 10 children?"
I simply cannot fathom the biology of it!

But then, in my darkest hour,
the answer is illuminated, written across the very sky
my heart's dearest close ranks about me
circling the wagons to deflect this worst of enemies

The magic and bounty of nine siblings
Each smart and kind, sensitive and savvy
Their spouses added to the mix for free
a bonus, a door prize if you will

All there for me
In sum, an inheritance unsurpassed
throughout the ages
An inheritance of kindred souls,
Ready to carry my palanquin for miles and miles

Mass-produced by two loving, old souls,
who scarcely knew the way
Through sheer doggedness and perseverance,
They created, unknowingly, a perfect
masterpiece of riches.

Flip-Flops are Great Equalizer
October 29, 2006

I'm pushing the envelope and wearing my flip-flops today, perhaps for the last time this year. I can feel Jack Frost nipping at my toes, but I'm reluctant to put them away for the season because they represent so much more than just comfort, utility and frugality.

I simply don't understand why people at the White House got so upset several months ago when some teenagers showed up wearing them. Perhaps they're too bourgeoisie for some of the patrician elements on both sides of the aisle in Washington. The story made me laugh.

Flip-flops represent everything that is great about this country. They are the great equalizer! Sure, Paris Hilton probably pays more for her flip-flops than I do for my Old Navy version, but who cares? In the end, she doesn't look any better (well, maybe a little) in her stylized version than any other size zero, emaciated blonde running around on the wrong side of the tracks in Brooklyn or the Bronx.

Just about everybody can afford flip flops in various colors, and whether they buy them at Saks Fifth Avenue or the Dollar Store, the effect is still the same, especially when paired with a skirt or other dressy attire: a kind of funky, hip, devil-may-care attitude that underlies the entire American experience. After all, let's not forget, our forefathers were all rebels and quite proud of it. Maybe that's what flip-flops remind me of the most.

Thoreau said it best in "Walden." "It is an interesting question how far men would retain their relative rank if they were divested of their clothes. Could you, in such a case, tell surely of any company of civilized men, which belonged to the most respected class?"

The same can certainly be said about shoes. It's hard to be snobby, or pretend you're really glamorous when instead of Jimmy Choos or Manolo Blahniks (who can walk in those anyway?), you wear flip-flops from Wal-Mart, just like everyone else in the room.

The only thing I don't like about flip-flops is that you really need to have a pedicure if you're going to wear them all summer and into winter. Like I do! But please, none of that French manicure nonsense—where the tip of your toe is painted bright white—with flip-flops. It kind of ruins the bohemian experience, don't you think?

The last time flip-flops were in vogue, I was in college and I loved them then, too. I had every color and style imaginable and wore them with everything. They were also perfect for a college student's budget. Back then we called them thongs—of course, that brings up an entirely different mental image today. It took my daughters a few weeks to cure me of that grotesque allusion to flip-flops.

On top of their patriotic allure, flip-flops are also darned convenient. If you leave your flip-flops behind at a family member's house, or at a sleepover, or leave them out in the rain—no worries. Forgot shoes altogether on a family vacation? No worries. Even gas stations and convenience stores have them in stock.

Lost one of your black flip-flops? Just root around in your daughter's, sister's, friend's, or neighbor's closet. Since black is always a fashion staple, everyonc is sure to have at least one black flip-flop. Even if the borrowed shoe is a slightly different size, who can tell? You can pair up a flip and a flop of slightly different sizes and shades, and no one will be the wiser.

In any case, I've found that most people are so worried about what they have on, that they never really notice what anyone else has on. I've also found that we all take ourselves way too seriously most of the time. But whenever I slide my feet into my favorite pair of flip-flops, they remind me that life really is too short to sweat the details.

Or as Thoreau says, "I am sure that there is greater anxiety, commonly, to have fashionable … clothes, than to have a sound conscience."

Amen brother!

Nov 9, 2006 11:27 am

I was in and out of Duke yesterday with no problems. Vaccine number seven and still going strong. Trying to stay well so we can stay on course with the last chemo scheduled for the week after Thanksgiving.

Getting paranoid about germs—a column to come on that topic!

Love,

Susan

Halloween Spooks Mom
November 11, 2006

I always breathe a big sigh of relief when Halloween is over. Give me the stress, expense and hard work of Christmas any day over the anxiety of helping my children figure out the perfect costume for Halloween. The proverbial "early bird" never wins in the costume game; almost without exception the little darlin' is sure to change his or her mind at the last minute. Still, I begin discussing our options early in October in order to narrow our focus, get the creative juices flowing, and assuage my neurotic, motherly tendency to be in total control.

I certainly have found myself in the position of frantically pawing through the leftover costumes on October 30th, but usually we don't resort to buying costumes, because the best ones are created from stuff around the house.

I remember creating Sacajawea's braids as a kid from my mom's old stockings and fringing the hem of an old brown skirt to create her dress. Or maybe my older sisters created these masterpieces and I merely pulled them from the trunk in the attic, a treasure chest full of all kinds of odds and ends and partial costumes, some expertly sewn by my paternal grandmother, others picked up at garage sales or handed down from older cousins.

In any case, fragments pulled from the trunk were sure to fire our imaginations. Creating a Halloween costume back then required careful planning, plotting and organizing – all done with minimal input and expense by Mom and Dad.

My youngest daughter seems to have inherited my views on dressing up. "I don't like those costumes from the store," she told me recently. "Don't you remember, Mom? I usually make up my own costumes," she declared, after I suggested, out of desperation and the dwindling number of days until Halloween, that we go to the store and buy a costume.

As I thought back over the last few years, I realized it was true. One year she took the easy route and went as a cheerleader. I was delighted the decision was made so effortlessly and thrilled to get some practical use out of the way-too-expensive, utterly nonsensical ensemble I had reluctantly purchased for her from a "tween" boutique. Last year she decided to dress up as an old lady, with a walker rescued from Grandma's attic. After her school choir performed at several nursing homes, she put the finishing touch on her costume: tennis balls on the front legs of the walker.

So this year I decided to give her artistic license and some breathing room. Really, I was just glad to be rid of the responsibility. As the days before the big trick-or-treating event waned, however, I realized there wasn't much "creating" going on around my house. I began making a few suggestions, hoping she would take the bait. But, no, my ideas, especially when it comes to costumes, are never good enough.

Finally, I used my foolproof backup plan: I enlisted (with the customary bribe) the help of Big Sister. Anything she suggests is always listened to, especially when it is delivered in a kind voice, totally atypical of the usual snide and sneering sibling attention dished out around here.

It worked like a charm. After a mere twenty minutes the nerd costume was gathered up, tried on and packed away for the school party. It certainly wasn't the best costume we've ever designed. In fact, Grandma asked on Halloween night, "Isn't she dressing up?" "She's already in her costume!" I responded emphatically, ignoring a nagging unease over the fact that Grandma couldn't tell the difference between her nerd costume and her everyday attire.

Of course, she froze her little tush off because she wouldn't wear a warm coat over her costume (but that's a subject for another day). Sniffling and coughing all over the neighborhood from a cold developed last week, she greedily emptied her sack of candy on her bedroom floor and sorted it out before falling exhausted into bed. The next day her cold was worse and she stayed home sick from school.

But at least we made it through another Halloween.

Decorating for Holiday Brings Happiness
November 12, 2006

Today I opened my first box of Christmas decorations. I know, I know, it's way too early to begin setting up for Christmas, but this year I am determined to enjoy it slowly, luxuriously, the way it should be enjoyed every year.

Last year I was miserable for most of December. Walking around with a pounding, throbbing in my head caused by a stage-four brain tumor the size of a lime makes everyday living something of a chore.

Still, I managed to get Christmas on the table, so to speak. I put up decorations, helped out with parties at school, shopped, wrapped gifts and carefully cleaned and mended slightly used toys and clothing to donate to charities. I just couldn't understand why I didn't feel the joy and beauty of the season like I usually do.

My childhood memories of Christmas are magical. Even with ten children in the house, our piles of toys under the tree were impressive. We never noticed that the bikes or baby beds had probably been repaired or repainted, or that the doll's clothes might have entertained a small stain created by some other girl in some other household. We only knew that we had more fun things in one morning than we would see the entire rest of the year.

I've always tried to maintain that sense of magic for my own children even though, as they get older, the cost of electronic items on their list makes for a shrinking pile of gifts under the tree.

Last January, my first thought upon hearing the grim news after my surgery was: My God, I have spent the last Christmas with my children and it was miserable! My thoughts flashed back to the hectic week before Christmas. Usually I start shopping early, trying to pick out special, yet practical, gifts for everyone on my list. But last year I found myself in the aisles of the large discount stores literally piling things into my cart with little regard for their intrinsic value. I simply knew I was running out of days and had to have something under the tree for all the names on my list.

Just several months later, many of those cheap items were thrown out or given away during a weekend spent diligently cleaning out the basement. This year I intend to go back to my original mode of shopping: slowly, carefully (albeit online!) while thanking the universe for each of the special people in my life.

Sorting through my decorations will also take me a lot longer this year. Friends and family members kindly packed them up while I recovered in the hospital after surgery that took place on January 6. How fitting that the date also marks the Epiphany, or the day the wise men arrived in Bethlehem to worship the newborn King. I always leave my decorations up until Gaspar, Melchior and Balthasar show up. Or maybe I just put off the mundane, somehow depressing task of abandoning the Christmas spirit for another year.

I wandered around the house for weeks in late January looking for my laundry baskets, finally finding them in the basement storage area, chock full of Christmas decorations randomly packed away. Of course, I ran out and bought new clothes baskets, content to save the sorting out for this year.

Lo, and behold, that time is now upon me. But I'm happy to commence with the holiday work a little early. I'm no longer freaked out about having spent my last Christmas with my girls. Despite the poor statistics surrounding my diagnosis, I still feel, perhaps naively, that I have many years ahead with my family.

But I don't intend to waste this Christmas by succumbing to needless stress or worry, or unnecessary obligations and responsibilities. I intend to savor it and treasure it as if it were indeed my last. For as my wise, older sister reminded me as she greeted me with a huge embrace upon my homecoming last year, "None of us knows how much time we have."

Perhaps we should all celebrate each Christmas as if it were our last.

Nov 15, 2006 8:14 pm

I'm enjoying writing my column again but spend most of my creative passion on that, so I'm not very good at updating you all. But I pretty much bare all by writing my columns!

Looking forward to visiting with family and friends over the holidays. I am feeling well, getting vitamin C infusions weekly to keep healthy, and head to Duke soon.

Love,
Susan

Thin Flattering, but Good Health Trumps Fashion
November 19, 2006

It's somewhat dismaying to be raising three daughters in a culture that values thinness in women almost above all else. This has been so ingrained in me, that even while battling a life-threatening illness, I still feel a heady glee over losing a large percentage of body fat. In oncology circles it's called cachexia, or a wasting away of the patient. In social circles, however, it's called something else.

"You look great," people frequently declare these days. This, of course, is a euphemism which can mean one of two things. "You look great—considering the hell you're putting your body through," or "Wow, you finally lost that middle-aged, belly-fat thing you had going on for awhile."

I have dropped many pounds since my diagnosis, first from surgery, next from sheer freaking out, then from the drudgery of chemotherapy, and finally, because I am trying to eat only that which will nourish my body and soul. (That was not me you saw at Dairy Queen last night eating a Peanut Buster Parfait—I swear!) I am certainly glad to have lost some weight, for even before my surgery I was falling victim to the encroaching pounds of age and a slowing metabolism. But it can be frustrating to say, "I have nothing to wear," and actually mean it.

When I returned home from the hospital last January, my youngest sister, who has done very well in the advertising and film business, sent me a beautiful silk scarf to wear around my partially shaved head. Later that week another, more practical sister was visiting. She picked up the new scarf from the heap of gifts. "This is a Valentino," she snapped. "If you're not going to wear this, you need to return it."

At that point my amazing sisters and in-laws were pretty much running my household, and so she packed it up, took it back to

St. Louis, and returned it to the department store. Then she took the money and hit the sale racks, returning the following week with bags of pants and shirts, all in my new size, and all for the price of one luxurious silk scarf, the exact price of which I have yet to ascertain.

I have since shrunk beyond that size as well and even though I am feeling great and very energetic, still I sometimes feel a nagging panic.

A few days after I took my first oral chemotherapy agent, I sat at the dinner table feeling thoroughly nauseated and listless. This, I thought with dismay, is why many people go straight downhill once they are on chemotherapy. For the first time in my entire life I was afraid I would not be able to eat enough calories to fuel my body, and that I would continue to shrink until all my strength and vigor were gone. Once that happens, I imagine it is easy to succumb to cancer, letting it finish off what is left of your body.

In the medical reports, many people die of cancer. In my heart, I know that many of them really die from the treatment. And so, although I am careful with my diet, believing that every illness should be first and foremost addressed with lifestyle changes, every now and then I do sneak off to Dairy Queen or pick up my favorite treat, a chocolate croissant, just to fatten myself up a little. After all, an occasional bit of "comfort" food can be healing as well.

Meanwhile, I like to strut a little in my new, slightly smaller jeans. I also feel stronger and healthier than I have in a really long time, thanks to my many alternative therapies, and my amazing yoga and bodypump instructors.

But mostly I'm just relieved to finally be down to my fighting weight, because I know I will have to be vigilant for whatever remains of my life span. "Bring it on!" is my new mantra.

By the way, you know those really skinny Victoria's Secret models, the ones with the huge you-know-whats? Well, that just ain't natural. Take it from one who knows—when your butt shrinks, so does everything else!

Nov 20, 2006 3:59 pm

Looking forward to the long Thanksgiving holiday, free of basketball games and practices and algebraic formulas to help figure out (Joe does that last one, not me). We leave for St. Louis on Wednesday to spend time with all the amazing O'Briens.

I have felt all the prayers and kind thoughts these last several months, but please remember me again next week as I complete my final round of chemotherapy. I begin Sunday evening and will be done on Thursday evening, just in time to enjoy a glass of wine with friends at my first Christmas party on Friday!

For anyone sick of hearing about cancer, I'm sorry. It's all I know how to write about for this moment.

Love you all,

Susan

Receiving Can Be Harder Than Giving
November 26, 2006

I am giving thanks this holiday weekend for all the special people in my life who have been so generous to me and my family over the past several months. But I have to confess, it has been extremely disconcerting to find myself constantly taking from others.

I come from a long line of givers. My parents always emphasized the importance of being self-sufficient, but they also stressed the importance of giving—to family first and then to church, school, community and neighbors, not necessarily in that order. We also never really had expensive things, so maybe that's why it was easier to pass items on to others. Whatever the reason, the habit has stuck.

As usual, our family Thanksgiving feast last week ended with the traditional exchange of "stuff."

"Hey, I've got a bag for you in the car," someone said as the coats began to appear from the back bedroom.

"Oh, I've got something for you too, that lamp you wanted from my basement."

"Well, don't leave before I give you those cushions you asked for," someone else hollered above the din.

Meanwhile, the husbands rolled their eyes and reluctantly piled more bags of stuff into the already loaded vehicles. These kinds of exchanges have been going on my entire life. A couple of years ago, my older sister astonished me by giving me something of great value without hesitation.

Sitting around her living room one evening, I casually remarked that I would probably buy a wedding band—fifteen years or so after taking my vows.

Having been a rebel in my younger years, I had scorned the traditional diamond and band in favor of a lovely, gold amethyst ring. At the time, my husband thought that was great (and way cheap) but over the years he began to drop hints that he wanted me to have a band. (Not a diamond?) I guess he was worried that without a wedding band I would be flirting in the produce aisle at Wal-Mart.

After expressing all of this to my sister that night, she immediately took the band off her left hand and said, "Here, do you want to wear Grandma's ring?"

I was utterly speechless, unaware that she even had my paternal grandmother's ring, the one my mother wore for many years, much to my father's chagrin, because it was wider and heavier than her own thin band. I slipped the well-worn, but still beautiful ring onto my own finger, and it fit perfectly. Tears welled up in my eyes. "I would love to wear this ring," I whispered.

"Well, take it," she insisted. "Mine is being resized, and I was just wearing it until I got mine back," she explained.

So, yes, I've been learning about giving my entire life.

But this past year I've been learning another lesson that is just as important, but sometimes harder to embrace: how to receive from others—especially strangers—with grace, humility and appreciation, not because we are pathetic or lack the skills to provide for ourselves, but because we are all part of the same universe and share the same joy and sadness, the same complex, incomprehensible human experience.

Deepak Chopra says in his book, "The Seven Spiritual Laws for Parents," that people must give away the very things they expect to receive in this world, whether that is money, time, compassion or mercy. "The giver is never the giver, just as the receiver is never the receiver. Both stand in for the [divine] spirit. Every time we receive, we are getting a glimpse of divine love. In every getting there is a spiritual lesson."

I have certainly learned many lessons through all of my "getting." I have been more uncomfortable than I can express, frequently moved even to tears by the generous gifts heaped upon me during my journey through cancer. But I have come to realize, in one of those funky epiphanies that only a crisis can invoke, that by accepting a gift from someone else, I am also helping them to realize their own "getting" of whatever the universe, or God, has in store for them.

So to all my benefactors—you're welcome!

Note:

I actually wrote this column before the holiday to meet my deadline, thereby missing another great anecdote to include in the piece. After Thanksgiving dinner we were sitting around the table at Therese and Bill's, the teapot had appeared and some of us were considering a second piece of pie, when Therese briskly walked up to the table and began wrapping up her Waterford goblets and boxing them up. "Jane, you take these home," she commanded. "They match the ones you have."

I guess we're all getting to that age when simplicity and "clean surfaces" become something of a siren's call. Nothing is sacred. Watch out kids and spouses!

Snow Days Bring Back Memories
December 3, 2006

Long after my childhood ended, I could still feel the excitement of a snow day embedded in my very marrow. Waking up to see all the sharp edges of the world blurred and covered over by the beauty of freshly fallen snow meant a day free from the boredom and drudgery of school. Whereas most days my mother had to call for me countless times before I finally dragged my weary body from bed, on a snow day I bounded up full of energy, ready to begin the day's adventures.

We were lucky enough to have a big hill just across the street and through the neighbor's back yard, close enough to make multiple forays throughout the long day. The family upon whose property the hill sat also owned a luxurious toboggan—the first one I had ever seen. Of course, they needed it because they had twelve children. When all the other neighborhood Catholic children, many of them with three or four siblings in tow, descended upon the spot, there was quite a party going on.

We all came from working-class families, so we didn't care if our gloves matched, or if our boots were worn or even waterproof. We would stay out sledding until our hands, feet and ears were entirely numb before finally conceding to common sense and heading back home for hot chocolate. During any season, my mother could never keep enough milk in the house to sate us; on snow days a gallon could be gone before breakfast.

Today I occasionally pass by my childhood sledding hill and remark upon how puny it appears. Back then it was grandiose and imposing and we rode our individual sleds down it, or piled on the toboggan in a tangled heap, bodies falling off right and left as the slick wooden vehicle raced down the slope.

In our adolescent years, "the hill" as we came to call it, took on a fresh allure—an opportunity to flirt with members of the opposite sex and even a chance to press flesh to flesh during our pile ups on the toboggan. Granted, we were all piled into bulky snow gear, but I still remember the thrill of my arm pressing against the coat sleeve of my latest crush as we whirled down the hill in a heap.

Years later, long before I had a family of my own, my mother recounted the other side, the dark side, of the snow-day experience.

"Oh, I always hated snow days," she moaned. "You kids would run around for an hour looking for enough gloves and hats and boots to go outside. Then you'd last about ten minutes before marching back inside and dropping all of your sopping-wet stuff onto the kitchen floor. Two hours later, you'd be starting the whole thing over again!" she exclaimed in exasperation.

I can still envision her small, turn-of-the-century kitchen with frozen garb strewn all over. Mud rooms hadn't even been invented yet, at least not in our neighborhood. Nevertheless, she patiently made us hot chocolate, and if she sulked or yelled, we were impervious to her complaints. Nothing could mar the perfection of a snow day!

Today I'm experiencing the dark side firsthand. Luckily we have a tiny mudroom off the kitchen, so our snow gear piles up there where we all trip over it going in and out of the house before finally hanging the wet gloves and scarves by the fireplace to dry, anticipating the next trip into the blinding wilderness.

Unlike my childhood self, my girls care intensely whether their gloves match, and they usually have ski pants and wonderful boots that are totally waterproof. I guess you could say they're spoiled in this regard, and in many others as well.

But I'm delighted to see they can still feel the magic and the giddiness of a snow day. Even our high-tech world of instant messaging and cell phones and iPods can't match in grandeur what Mother Nature occasionally rolls out to spark in some long-forgotten inner place, the wonder and magic and innocence of childhood.

An Ode to Joyless Christmas Ballet

The Previous Year

My wish for you this Christmas season is not for world peace (although I'm not personally against such a notion), but rather for something much more pragmatic. I certainly wish you a season of peace and joy, but also one without having to endure a single performance of "The Nutcracker."

Don't get me wrong. I love the idea of "The Nutcracker"! It's just that in reality the performance never delivers what the audience, especially children, expect—namely a story they can sink their teeth into. With almost no dialogue, who can even follow the storyline? And more importantly, who wants to follow the storyline? Watching a nutcracker fight off gigantic mice is considerably passé for a generation raised on the likes of "Star Wars" and Harry Potter.

A few years ago, falling prey to the allure of "The Nutcracker" ballet, I purchased tickets for an expensive performance in St. Louis. My daughters and I dressed up, drove three hours and entered the auditorium with excitement. Within the first thirty minutes, however, just after Herr Drosselmeyer presented the nutcracker to his goddaughter, Clara, my youngest daughter turned to me and whispered, "Is it almost over?"

I looked down the row of seats at my other daughters and their female cousins, who had also attended the performance, and was dismayed to see their eyes glazing over with boredom. One of them was yawning while the rest were fidgeting in their seats and peering at their programs, counting down the musical numbers until intermission. And I felt exactly the same way.

I looked around at the other people in the theatre. They seemed interested in the production, but perhaps they were just better at hiding their boredom than we were. Or perhaps they drank a double espresso just before taking their seats. That would certainly help give one the appearance of paying attention.

"Why don't they serve wine at this performance?" I desperately asked the usher.

The junky concession snacks we purchased and consumed during the intermission somewhat alleviated our boredom. Yet we still filed desultorily back into the auditorium feeling something akin to dread.

At least the Sugar Plum Fairy is coming up soon, I thought. Surely she will dispel our disappointment.

But the sight of all those super-slim ballerinas prancing around and contorting their bodies gracefully only made me feel terrible about that Crunch bar I had wolfed down during the break, in the hope that the resulting sugar buzz would keep me from dozing off before the end of the performance.

Apparently Tchaikovsky, in addition to composing all of the music for "The Nutcracker," wrote a shorter version of the ballet, but, unfortunately, the longer (much, much longer) version is the one that persists today. I think the audience should get a sticker after suffering through the entire performance, something that says, "I survived 'The Nutcracker'!" or "I made it through the entire thing!"

The original story, published in 1816 by E.T.A. Hoffman, was a "dark and morbid" story, never intended for children, but rather designed to "show the depraved and desperate side of mankind." Now that sounds interesting.

I think their version of depraved, however, has been much watered down in the almost 200 years since the original story was published. Meanwhile, modern audiences have been entertaining themselves with the likes of "The Texas Chainsaw Massacre." Obviously, even the aberrant mice in the first act can't top that kind of thrill.

About the only thing we could relate to in the first act is when Clara's bratty brother, Fritz, breaks the nutcracker in a jealous fit.

Still not as interesting as Harry Potter fighting Lord Voldemort, but at least we could figure out what was going on during that part of the ballet. After all, that kind of drama is something we're used to seeing at our house almost daily. Without the pirouettes, of course.

One thing I did get out of the ballet was the opportunity to name drop.

"Yes, we were in St. Louis seeing 'The Nutcracker,'" I would casually announce at a neighborhood Christmas party. No need to mention that I merely endured it, of course. That would only dispel the impression I was hoping to make of being a cultured, intelligent, interesting person.

"Yes, that was the first (and last!) time my girls have seen the ballet."

Luckily, no one asked my daughters how they liked it. I'm afraid their responses would have given us away immediately as what we truly are—way too bourgeois to enjoy the production.

"It was so long," one would blurt out.

"It was so boring," another one would add.

"I couldn't figure out what was going on," the last one would chime in.

"Amen," I would silently add.

Next year perhaps we'll go see something more closely aligned with my mood. "Scrooge" should be just about right.

Christmas Lights a Messy Tangle
December 17, 2006

Forget everything I said or wrote a few weeks back about savoring each and every minute of Christmas. That was before I opened my fourth or fifth box of decorations, the ones with the Christmas lights in them. Suddenly I'm a total Scrooge again.

The first box of lights I opened contained a tangled mess of multiple strands all twisted around each other—pure chaos. Carefully, I unhooked the plugs and meticulously separated each of the lines, and then plugged them in to see if they worked, before hanging them (Rule Number 1).

Of course, half of the strands worked perfectly, and the other half only worked for half the string.

I know, it sounds like some kind of torturous, word-problem: if frustrated parents have two beers while figuring out the Christmas lights, and only half the lights work on half the strands, how long will it take said parents to throw them all away, drive to the store and buy all new lights?

Answer: It's a trick question.

Everyone knows it takes at least three or four beers to really get the hang of Christmas lights (Rule Number 2). I consider myself to be fairly intelligent, but I cannot for the life of me troubleshoot and repair strands of Christmas lights that are on the fritz.

I know it has something to do with blown fuses, so of course I regret throwing those extra fuses away with the packaging from last year. Still, I figure a person with half a brain (no pun intended) should be able to figure out how to get all the lights to work.

My husband has many interests and hobbies but detangling lights isn't one of them, so he's not much help in this situation.

Although he's smart enough not to verbalize it, I'm sure he's thinking, What's the point of going to all the trouble and expense of putting lights on the house just for a few weeks?

In this regard, I'm sure he's not alone. I've commiserated with many friends whose husbands feel exactly the same way about decorating the house for the holidays.

So, instead of nagging my reluctant husband this year (Rule Number 3), I did what I always do when I have a question, I Googled it. I was determined not to throw away perfectly good lights just because half of them didn't work! Never mind that I already have about a gross of them stashed in the basement.

Carefully, I typed in replace + fuse + Christmas lights.

Out of the many selections that popped up I landed on someone's blog. After scanning through page after page of minute instructions I came to the meat of the issue:

"Most manufacturers hope you'll just throw the old lights away and buy new ones."

Okay, I give up already.

After stashing the old strands in the trash can, we brought out the ladder and proceeded to string the lights. Being too impatient to halt our project until we could make a run to the store to replace the faulty strands, we simply decided to put fewer lights on the house. That was probably a good idea anyway.

Last year we disregarded the instructions on the box and strung way too many strands together to outline our porch, resulting, of course, in blown fuses and half the lights going out immediately.

By limiting the number of strands we strung together this year, we became compliant with the directions from the manufacturer (Rule Number 4).

We also remembered to locate the male end close to the electric socket and the female end ready to connect to the next strand (Rule Number 5).

On more than one occasion I have stepped back to survey my handiwork only to realize I had no method for actually plugging the lights in because the entire strand had to be reversed.

So, I'm making my first New Year's resolution early. I'm done hoarding old Christmas lights in the hope that someday I'll be able to understand and fix them. Even with a whole brain, that seems beyond my intellectual capability.

Christmas Past Leaves a Week to Relax, Reflect The Previous Year

Finally, it's all over. The week between Christmas and the New Year has, in recent years, become my favorite part of the Christmas season, ever since I crossed over to the side of those who whine and complain about how much work Christmas is.

I never used to feel that way. I have only the happiest of memories from my childhood Christmases. They were magical and relaxed and fun in a way that nothing in adult life ever matches.

But after having a family of my own and succumbing to the countless holiday obligations and responsibilities of children, school and church, it struck me one holiday season, that behind the scenes of all those happy childhood memories, someone, namely my mother, was working her tail off to pull it all together!

Now that someone is me, and I am less than amused.

There simply is too much work to do in the few weeks of December. I've already jettisoned the tasks that don't really matter to me. I don't bake hundreds, or even dozens, of Christmas cookies and for the past several years I have given up on Christmas cards altogether.

Instead, I focus all my energies on what is, by most accounts, the least important part of Christmas: the shopping, wrapping and gift-giving.

Long gone are those peaceful hours spent during the holidays leisurely writing Christmas cards to long-lost friends while sipping a cup of hot tea. I used to enjoy wrapping presents and creating a kind of artwork with beautiful paper and bows. Alas, these days, the piles of presents are simply too big to linger over any one gift.

"We picked names during basketball practice and we're going to exchange presents at our next practice," my eldest daughter announces one day when I pick her up from school. "We can't spend more than a dollar," she continues. "Will you take me to Dollar Tree to do my shopping?"

It will cost more than a dollar for the gas to drive over there, I'm thinking, but still hanging on to a mere shred of Christmas spirit I don't say that.

The list of what I didn't get done this holiday season goes on and on, but still is much shorter than the list of what I actually did accomplish: shopped for, purchased and wrapped about 75 gifts; baked and cooked items to contribute to several family and neighborhood dinners and parties (after hosting Thanksgiving dinner for 25); wrote a handful of Christmas cards; put up the Christmas tree; decorated the house; listened to countless Christmas CDs; sat through our school's musical program (vocal and instrumental); helped my children study for multiple finals (ask me anything about the ...), all the while continuing the daily grind of writing, cooking, washing dishes and clothes, reading bedtime stories, checking hair for lice (but that's another story altogether), and driving my children all over creation.

And I accomplished most of it with gracious aplomb.

In fact, it wasn't until the last few days before Christmas that I began to get a little testy, a little frenzied. And by then, who could tell? Everyone I encountered was in the same boat—feeling slightly panicky about not being able to find the latest Xbox or iPod or cell phone.

But now, none of that matters anymore.

Sanity has returned to our household, and even though I will probably spend the next week running to the store for yet more batteries, and reading too many instruction manuals for all the new games and toys Santa brought, toys that will probably, despite my husband's exactitude in putting them together, work for only a few brief hours before breaking irreparably, I will find time to read and relax this week and perhaps even take a nap in between breaking down boxes and throwing away bits of plastic and wrapping paper, and beginning, bit by bit, to dismantle all of the holiday decorations.

Finally, I'll have time to sit down and watch "Scrooge," the musical starring Albert Finney—the very best production ever of Charles Dickens's "A Christmas Carol." I may even get around to writing a few more "New Year's cards," as I have come to call them.

Of course, I'll also have to begin organizing the pile of gifts that need to be returned and searching for all the necessary receipts (luckily, I save every one). But even that daunting task coupled with taking down my outside Christmas lights won't deflate my burgeoning Christmas spirit. Hip, hip hooray! It's all over for another year!

I guess I don't need to watch "Scrooge." I've become Scrooge! Bah, humbug!

Germ War Tactics Get Refined
December 31, 2006

I've never been a germ fanatic. I've been reading about alternative medicine and holistic healing for many years, so I have come to believe that a healthy body and immune system will ward off most invading germs and viruses. But as we head into the cold and flu season this year, I am, to use my daughter's expression, freaking out!

With depressed white blood counts and platelets due to medical treatment, I am paranoid about getting sick. Suddenly I realize that all the things I touch throughout the day have been touched before me by hundreds of people with millions of germs. Shopping carts, ATM buttons, gas pumps, door handles, yoga mats and barbells at the gym have all been contaminated countless times over by complete strangers.

I know, I know—I sound completely crazy. Quite frankly, I'm surprised I haven't literally worried myself sick! I just can't help it.

All of my senses are heightened. That person behind me in the airplane hacking away surely has pneumonia or whooping cough! That kid just wiped her nose with her hand and now she's handing me her glass! That clerk just took gum out of his mouth and threw it in the trash can before counting out my change!

"Did you wash your hands?" I frequently snap at my children (and occasionally, my husband).

I've taken to marking my water bottles at home with a bold "S" in the hope that no one will drink out of them without my knowing.

I've also taken an acute interest in the layout of public bathrooms. I always appreciate the ones you can escape without using your hands after they've been washed, and have become quite adept at pushing down the towel-dispenser handle using my elbow, and triggering the door handle using some article of clothing to shield my clean hand. I just love it when the trash can is strategically placed next to the door so I can use my paper towel to grip the door handle before discarding it.

Hands down, my triple-star bathroom rating goes to the rest areas along Interstate 70. The new hand-washing contraptions dispense soap, warm water and then hot air in quick succession. Furthermore, the doors always push out easily with a hip or forearm.

About a month ago, my daughter woke up in the middle of the night with the flu. I frantically fled the basement guest room to find cleaner accommodations above, leaving my husband to nurse her and clean up.

I felt absolutely no guilt whatsoever. In fact, I felt a rather perverse sense of satisfaction as I told them goodnight, remembering the countless times I had found myself in exactly the same situation when our kids were young. I remember stripping them out of their pajamas, both of us half asleep, then stripping the bed and remaking it all the while soothing them and assuring them that everything was fine, and secretly praying that we wouldn't have to repeat the entire episode an hour later.

At Mass we used to hold hands to recite the "Lord's Prayer" but that practice has been discontinued lately. Still, at a recent Mass to celebrate Grandparent's Day our priest encouraged everyone to join hands.

Reluctantly, I clasped the hands of the two children on either side of me, pressing their small, plump, moist palms against my own. But I wasn't reciting the "Lord's Prayer."

Instead, I think I mumbled something like, "My Lord, forgive me for wondering exactly where these hands have been and quickly deliver me into the bathroom to wash my sullied hands so that I can become worthy and clean enough to accept thy Communion wafer and transfer it into my mouth, without being infected with bubonic plague. Amen."

I've experimented with all kinds of gestures designed to avoid shaking hands with someone while mumbling something about "blah, blah, sick, blah, blah." Sometimes they respond emphatically: "Oh, I'm not worried about getting sick!"

"Yes, but I am," I silently respond. "More than you could ever imagine."

Despite my maniacal anxiety, I have somehow, miraculously, managed to stay healthy. For now. How many months until spring?

4

Be still and know that I am...

— *Psalm 46:10*

Reflections
January 2007

Catching on to a new year has always been difficult for me. The first dozen times I write a check or date an official form in January and February, I inevitably cling to the old year. It takes me weeks to finally get it through my thick head that the number has changed.

But not this year. I guess I couldn't wait to shake the dust of 2006 off my proverbial boots, because I haven't once mistakenly written 2006 on a check or document.

I've never been one for deep New Year's reflections. I always figure those kinds of introspective moments should be carried out on an ongoing basis all year round. But this past year has been a dramatic and traumatic one for my family. I'm sometimes tempted to give in to the cliché that it's been the worst year of my life.

But I feel that words have tremendous power, not only to influence others, but also to influence the way the speaker or the writer thinks and feels. That's why I haven't been able to use the word "sick" this past year. I've always preferred other phrases, like "since my surgery," or "since my diagnosis," rather than "since I got sick." The fact is, other than a few weeks after my surgery, I haven't really felt sick. By refusing to use that expression, I think I've kept a mental image of health alive in my mind and in my heart.

In the same way, I can't say that this has been the worst year of my life. Surely it's been one of the most difficult, but there have been so many good things that have come out of the year, many of which I've written about the past several months.

Ultimately, I don't think one can declare a year that profoundly changes everything about you to be a bad one.

While boxing up some old books recently, I came across the dozens of titles that kind friends and family members had purchased for me immediately after my diagnosis. I quickly scanned through many of them, gleaning bits and pieces of crucial information from all of them, at a time when I was desperate for a glimmer of optimism.

"Are you ever going to write about anything other than cancer?" my husband asked me one evening as he peered over my shoulder.

At the time I wondered if anything else would ever interest me.

Now that I am almost back to my normal life, I find I'm interested in writing about many other topics again. Still, I have much to say about cancer, so please excuse me as I continue to occasionally insert a column on that topic.

Toxic Legacy Stalks Children
Eighteen Months Earlier

Yeah, I bought the breast cancer stamps. Paid eight cents extra to mail my bills and letters, and I was glad to do it.

But I'm quite certain that no matter how many stamps we buy at an inflated price, our chances of beating breast cancer are slim to none, as long as we continue to dump carcinogenic materials into our homes, our offices, our gardens, and, most disastrously, into our children.

Even before they are born, our children are chock full of chemicals, many of them deemed carcinogenic, according to a recent report released by the Environmental Working Group (EWG), a relatively small, but apparently influential research and lobbying group.

The study found "an average of 200 industrial chemicals and pollutants in umbilical cord blood from 10 babies" chosen at random in the United States. Of the total 287 chemicals detected, "180 cause cancer in humans or animals, 217 are toxic to the brain and nervous system, and 208 cause birth defects or abnormal development in animal tests."

Furthermore, researchers concluded they would have found many more chemicals in these same babies, but "laboratories have yet to develop methods to test human tissues for the vast majority of chemicals on the market."

In fact, of the 75,000 chemicals currently being used and marketed in America, 63,000 were grandfathered in as safe by the 1976 Toxic Substances Control Act (TSCA), despite the fact that these chemicals have had no "safety scrutiny," according to the EWG report. Among these potentially harmful substances are many "hormone-mimicking chemicals like dioxins" which can lead to breast cancer.

Little wonder, then, that the rate of invasive female breast cancer surged upward by about twenty-five percent between 1973 and 1996, according to the report. Researchers estimate this upward shift will continue and the occurrence of breast cancer could change from affecting one in seven women to one in four in a couple of generations.

Meanwhile, occurrence of childhood cancers has also risen dramatically, in some cases by as much as 68 percent, according to the report. It comes as no surprise then, that 80 to 90 percent of all cancers are linked to the environment rather than genetics, according to the National Cancer Institute.

Other childhood ailments, such as autism and attention deficit disorder, are also increasing at alarming rates, perhaps because of unrelenting exposure of babies and very small children to a plethora of chemicals that are many times more toxic to tiny bodies than they are to adults.

Scary statistics, scary enough to make me try to clean up my own environment.

Some of my friends laugh at me because I try to garden organically and disavow the use of commercial herbicides.

"It's totally safe. You can drink the stuff," insists a friend of mine who works in agriculture.

Thanks, but I'll stick to my chardonnay.

I also don't spray my home for bugs very often, putting up with the insult and inconvenience of ants in my kitchen and carpenter bees on my porch every spring.

My cleaning supplies are mostly non-toxic, so my house may be slightly less sanitized than most, but I figure the germs and the dirt are probably better than the chemicals, which is why I also suggest to my daughters that they avoid the hand sanitizers at school in favor of old-fashioned hand washing.

Finally, I try to buy organic foods whenever possible.

Much good my efforts will do me, however, when I'm surrounded by toxic chemicals: flame retardants in my furniture, computers and televisions; stain and grease resistors in my carpet and food wraps.

I know we can't do without chemicals, but I do expect the Environmental Protection Agency to do what most of us assume it has been doing all along, research the safety of new chemicals before they come on the market.

Apparently, however, that is not how things work. In reality, the EPA has little authority to require safety testing and when companies perform their own testing, large portions of the results can be held back from the government to protect a company's "confidential" information, according to the EWG report.

Rachel Carson, considered by some to be the mother of the modern environmental movement, predicted dire consequences from this deluge of chemicals in 1962 when she published "Silent Spring."

"Can anyone believe it is possible to lay down such a barrage of poisons on the surface of the earth without making it unfit for all life?" she asked. "This pollution is for the most part irrecoverable; the chain of evil it initiates … is for the most part irreversible," she wrote.

Perhaps it's finally time to begin listening to her message. Perhaps an ounce of prevention really is worth a pound of cure.

Cancer Drugs Missed Blessing
January 7, 2007

Now that I am officially done with chemotherapy, I have to set the record straight about why I have been better able to handle the caustic drugs that devastate so many others.

In reality, I have done well through my treatment, and better than many of my peers undergoing the same Duke University clinical trial.

However, the reason, while certainly bolstered by my "clean" living, is actually that through divine intervention, serendipity, or just plain dumb luck, about the only chemotherapy agent that is known to reliably penetrate the blood-brain barrier also happens to be one of the relatively less toxic ones. This, the doctors tell me, also happens to be the reason patients with my type of tumor, glioblastoma-multiforme, typically have such poor, long-term survival rates.

But I see the situation as an amazing opportunity.

I always believed that if faced with cancer I would never choose chemotherapy. Having been on a holistic health kick for about ten years now, I just didn't believe that you could attack cancer by first poisoning your body.

"So, why do you have cancer if you've been living so healthily?" you might ask. Believe me, I've been asking it plenty!

Over the past year, however, I've identified many areas in my life that have been out of whack, and have come to the obvious conclusion that cancer is an extremely complex disease, rarely based just on one physiological problem. Initially, though, I was profoundly disappointed.

As I researched my treatment options after being diagnosed, I wondered what good all my healthy living had done for me. I would walk out of ballgames or movies and see people smoking Marlboros and guzzling Mountain Dews and wonder why they didn't have cancer instead of me.

As Americans, we wouldn't dare pour Coke, or aspartame or Doritos into the gas tanks of our brand new BMWs or Escalades, and yet we routinely dump such sordid substances into machinery vastly superior in design and complexity—our bodies.

Even worse, we routinely dump the same toxic substances down the throats of our children.

Then, when we get sick, we pour even more poison down our throats in an effort to quickly reverse diseases that have probably taken years to manifest themselves.

I continued to rage against my fate and the standard western protocol for cancer as I wrestled with my treatment decisions, still reluctant to take chemotherapy.

But as I tucked my 9-year-old into bed each night, I realized that the decision was not just mine to make. My health, or lack thereof, could invoke immeasurable sadness and hardship upon the people I loved the most.

After much research and hand-wringing, coupled with many tears and prayers, I agreed to six months of temozolomide, primarily because it would give me access to the vaccine trial at Duke, where the vaccine would boost my body's own immune system's ability to eradicate the disease. That theory made much more sense to me than toxic drugs.

The fact that Temodar is relatively benign also weighed heavily in my decision. Most patients don't lose their hair and continue to work and perform their daily routines while on the medicine.

I concluded, therefore, that the drug might actually help me, only because it probably would not be strong enough to kill me first, allowing me to use my alternative modalities to keep me strong and cancer free. And that is exactly how it has worked out thus far.

People ask me if I'm now in "remission," but I'm not sure that's a term used by brain-tumor doctors. We have a sort of unwritten code because the statistics are so dire: "Don't ask; don't tell!"

For now, however, we are all delighted that I am still here and feeling good and living my life.

Sure, the poisonous drug I took out of desperation may, in fact, have halted the progression of my cancer for a brief time, but I know it is my ten years of healthy living that have ultimately saved me.

And I'm saddened that most oncologists, in their frantic search for a pharmaceutical cure for cancer, seem to have forgotten their primary rule: First, do no harm.

Jan 11, 2007 1:19 pm

Happy New Year to everyone. I am so glad to start a new year! We broke ground on our house addition yesterday so we are very excited and busy trying to make lots of decisions.

I am feeling great, started back into yoga this week and body pump class is kicking my butt after three weeks off over the holidays. I received the most heavenly organic dark chocolate ginger cookies—my new favorite! Simple pleasures truly are the best.

Meanwhile, we're all about basketball here.

Love,

Susan

Small Town Shopping Better Than Mall Hubbub
January 14, 2007

Like many others, I have been excitedly watching construction of the new shopping center west of town. Growing up in St. Louis, I became used to having a wide selection of commercial enterprises to patronize.

After moving to Sedalia more than fifteen years ago, I spent much time, too much time, lamenting all the things Sedalia didn't have: a variety of fine restaurants, large department stores, funky used bookstores, and multiple performing arts venues.

Ironically, I find lately, now that we are getting more chain stores, I feel ambivalent about the changes occurring here, and all across America.

This summer our family took a road trip to spend a week at the beach in South Carolina. Our trip was smooth and uneventful, except for the usual sibling squabbles, but I was unprepared for the vast change in America's landscape. I guess it's been a long time since I've taken a road trip of this magnitude, seventeen hours and 1,100 miles. Obviously, this is not the kind of trip you take when you've got toddlers in tow!

As we rolled into every town of any size I was dismayed to see that almost every shopping center looked exactly the same, with similar big-box stores: Barnes and Noble, Old Navy, Marshalls, Pier One, Target, Panera, Starbucks, etc.

On the one hand, it made being in a strange town somewhat more comfortable. We knew we could find something if we needed it, and were even able to do a lot of our back-to-school shopping while en route to the beach. And yes, I had plenty of Starbucks lattes to keep me awake while driving.

On the other hand, I found the shopping experience to be a little too comfortable! We ended up having the exact same shopping experience we could have had in Kansas City, St. Louis or even Columbia, Missouri, with a little southern twang thrown in.

So, I thought, what's the point of all this travel?

After all, the whole purpose of leaving home is to broaden your horizons and get out of your comfort zone. That's pretty hard to do today in much of America.

On my rather frequent trips to St. Louis to visit doctors or family members, I have begun to feel assaulted by the continuous encroachment of the big boxes on the countryside, with the accompanying insult of added traffic, noise and signage.

Every trip, I notice with increasing dismay that the urban sprawl continues to creep westward. Eventually Kansas City and St. Louis may be linked by a continuous line of huge retailers all vying for our hard-earned dollars.

So, instead of focusing on what Sedalia doesn't have these days, I'm counting my blessings. At the end of my trips, I now look forward to coming home to our sleepy town, where you can easily travel the streets without traffic at any time of day or night, and where we still have wide open spaces to enjoy.

And I'm actually glad that my three daughters can't engage in shopping as a recreational sport because we don't have huge malls. When my city sisters complain about their teens dragging them all over to find a coat or a swimming suit, I simply smile. At my house my girls know, either you find one during the few hours we spend at the mall, or you find it online. Even paying extra for shipping doesn't diminish the pleasure I feel at skipping all those exhausting and boring hours at the mall, and it still costs me less than all the frivolous, impetuous purchases we get lured into making while browsing.

Sure, I enjoyed shopping when I was younger, but now that I'm buying clothing, personal items, groceries and household stuff for the entire family, I've had enough!

Frankly, I don't care if I ever see the inside of another mall—except, of course, for the bookstores. The transition has taken a long time, but I guess I'm finally through whining and complaining about small-town living.

I guess I've become a country girl, through and through.

Jan 18, 2007 2:24 pm

After a long weekend hunkered down because of ice, and an unexpected snow day on Tuesday, I was extremely relieved to pack the kids off to school on Wednesday morning. We've had many basketball games cancelled this past week, so the makeup schedule will be brutal.

We head back to Duke on Monday for another vaccine and the leukapharesis procedure whereby they harvest my white blood cells to create more vaccine.

I am feeling well and strong. Enjoying the last, tenacious bloom on my Amaryllis bulb—a deep ruby red. When it fades, I guess the holidays will be officially over!

Love,

Susan

Parents Teach Early Lesson
January 21, 2007

As the curtain slid open, I was backstage feeling terrified. Most of the details of this particular performance are hazy, lost in the mind of a nervous 6-year-old child.

The year was 1965 and I was in school for the first time. I can't even remember what the performance was, but I presume, since the school was attached to a Catholic Church, that we were performing the Christmas pageant.

I vaguely remember that I was dressed up as a shepherd, or perhaps a sheep. I'm not even sure I had a line. I do remember, however, that when I walked on stage, the crowd erupted in uproarious laughter and my anxiety turned to confusion and bewilderment.

Why on earth are they laughing so hard? I wondered. This was certainly no comedy. That much I knew!

It was many years later when it occurred to me that their laughter must have spontaneously erupted at the strange sight of one lone, pale white face appearing suddenly in the midst of a dozen black ones.

Yes, I was one of only a couple of white students in my kindergarten class at Holy Angels Catholic school, located in an extremely poor neighborhood called Kinloch, which bordered my own lily-white, working-class neighborhood of Ferguson in suburban St. Louis. Long before the term was even coined, my mother was experimenting with a kind of reverse busing policy.

For years I never thought much about what had prompted my parents to send me to Kinloch, the very first predominantly black city in Missouri, incorporated in 1948, despite the fact that a perfectly good kindergarten, full of Caucasian children, existed just two blocks from my home.

It was only as I grew older, after both my mother and father had died, that I became acutely interested in their motivation, which, of course, was quite obvious.

In 1965 the Civil Rights Movement was in full throttle. My mother's older brother, George, traveled south to march with thousands of other activists in Selma, Alabama, where Martin Luther King, Jr. addressed the crowd of 25,000. Later that year Congress would pass the Voting Rights Act, which would dramatically increase the number of blacks who were eligible to vote.

My parents, stuck at home with ten children, a mortgage, jobs, housework and no money, nevertheless, found a means of voicing their opinion, of offering their support, by making a kind of foot soldier of what they cared for most in the world—their child.

I don't remember much else about my kindergarten experience in Kinloch, but the sight of the tarpaper shacks we passed en route has been seared into my memory forever.

When we occasionally attended church there as a family, the African-American women looked pretty much the same as the women in my neighborhood Catholic church, with hats respectfully covering their heads and pencil slim skirts with tailored jackets or sweater sets to match.

But the streets and houses were different from anything I had yet experienced, conveying clearly, even to my naïve and unlettered mind, the evidence of great poverty and the cruelty of fate.

All of these memories have been much on my mind this past week as I've read and thought about the great leaders, like Martin Luther King, Jr., who galvanized a vast movement across our nation.

But I've also thought with awe and astonishment of people like my mother and father, people who quietly rebelled against an unjust system by sending their 6-year-old to a black school in a lousy neighborhood.

I'm sure their decision seemed ludicrous or even ornery to some of their neighbors or acquaintances. But despite the risk of social condemnation, they followed their hearts.

Edmund Burke once said, "All that is necessary for the triumph of evil is that good men do nothing."

I'm glad my parents and so many others of their generation chose to do something. And even though I've forgotten much about my integrated kindergarten experience, the impact of it remains in my intellect, my heart, and my soul.

Perhaps that's what my parents were shooting for all along.

Jan 25, 2007 2:15 pm

Should have called all the O'Briens before writing my latest column about Dad and his garage. I'm sure we all have special memories of him—I'm certainly loving mine right now.

We're off to Duke on Monday again. Glad to get out of the construction zone. We're a dusty mess right now with demolition going on, but it is very exciting, too. It's going to be fantastic when it is all done.

Had another MRI done today, hope to get good news; will keep everyone posted.

Love,

Susan

Garages, Fathers Just Go Together
January 28, 2007

What a luxury—to have a nice roomy garage during the kind of icy, nasty weather that hit us the past two weekends.

I never really thought much about garages. Even when we built our house twelve years ago, I didn't much care about having one. Because I grew up in an old, turn-of-the-century home, I always thought a nice, big garage was something of a luxury.

Before we had a garage, my husband was always the one to go outside at 6 a.m. and scrape off the windshields of both our cars, so what did I need a garage for?

During our recent ice storm, though, I felt like royalty, able to park my van in a dry garage, knowing my car would be ice-free when next I came to claim it.

As I pulled my car in and out of this protected space during the winter storm, I thought more than once of my father.

More than anyone I have ever known, my Dad revered his garage. He loved to tinker with his vehicles, and his tiny old garage was a safe haven for him, a place he could escape to when the chaos of the house became too much for him. He was raised as an only child and often talked about the loneliness of that household. Still, I think he got more than he bargained for when he ended up with ten children.

By working on the car, he was constructively employed with familial duties, but safely away from the fray of the household. So naturally, we frequently saw the hood of the car up, my father happily bent over the engine lubricating, twisting, tweaking and adjusting. He always seemed happy and at peace in this domain.

The garage was so small that there really wasn't even room for the car to be parked there. Shelves had been built along three walls and were packed with coffee cans full of various sized nails and screws, oil cans, gas cans, tools for working on automobiles, and, of course, his precious carpenter tools.

As kids, we were often invited into this sanctuary. In fact, my father always tried to interest us in how the engine worked or how to change the oil filter or fix a flat tire. I know he was trying to empower his many daughters who would someday leave his home and his protection and might need such skills. But we were young and uninterested and frequently tuned him out when he began lecturing on his latest topic.

I did, however, pick up the bit about checking the oil, a skill I would need in later years since most of my cars, even into early adulthood, were "previously owned" jalopies that tended to drink a lot of oil.

Because of budget constraints, my husband and I went ten years without a garage after building our house. Finally, my husband got fed up with clearing off windshields every morning and decided it was time to build one.

Soon after the new garage was finished, I stumbled upon some old iron letters at an antique store and purchased my dad's initials, WTO (William Thomas O'Brien).

I placed them on the ledge of one of the windows, trying to ignore the nagging thought that my father would be appalled at the state of my garage. He ran a tight ship with everything in its proper place. Conversely, my garage has become a kind of dumping ground for everything we don't know what to do with—and occasionally a raccoon that gets in through the cat door and wreaks havoc on the recycling bins, the cat food or anything else smelling remotely edible.

Gradually we're adding more storage cabinets and one day I fully intend for my garage to be neat as a pin, the kind of place my father would have loved and proudly maintained.

In the meantime, though, I just kick the basketballs and scooters out of my way and pray I don't run over anything important (like the cat) as I ease my minivan inside, shutting out the icy blasts from the world outside.

Cookies Fun to Buy, Not Sell
February 4, 2007

For the first time in several years there are no Girl Scout cookies being sold at my house—no cases of Thin Mints to off-load at the local Scout camp; no stacks of cookies in my garage, carefully compiled and double-checked awaiting the arrival of the girls and their parents who will have to unpack, sort and deliver the cookies to their eager customers; no paperwork and cash piling up on my kitchen counter.

Instead, I am on the other side of the aisle, graciously ordering boxes of Peanut Butter Patties, Shortbreads or Thin Mints, knowing that all I have to do is write a check when the cookies arrive on my doorstep.

We have great memories of Girl Scouting, but cookie sales are certainly not among them.

For many years I was in the thick of the cookie madness. I never volunteered to chair the cookie drive; I was too chicken for that! But most years I helped out wherever and whenever I could, grumbling whenever I encountered a slacker sales team, who failed to tally and double-check their order sheet before handing it in.

Each year, families can start selling only after the big "cookie rally" occurs. Of course, I complied with this rule, but I did find it helpful to drop a few hints to our best customers, letting them know, "the cookies are coming!" In other words, save your order for us.

I also began keeping the order forms from previous years so that I could hit up the big buyers first thing, before some other controlling mom could get to them, and I learned to delete from the call list those who ordered only one box. Sorry, but that just doesn't seem worth the effort, not when your goal is to sell 200 boxes because your daughter is intent on winning that plastic monkey manufactured in China for fifty cents.

If you're unlucky enough to have more than one Scout, each with a troop quota of 200—well, you're in big trouble. You better have made some serious cold calls long before the infamous cookie rally, 'cause Uncle Bob and Aunt Hazel are never going to order enough to bail you out.

I know in a perfect world my daughters would traipse all over creation personally making each and every sale, but one of my most traumatic childhood memories involves wandering around the neighborhood, desperately trying to sell books of Easter Seals to people who had no qualms about mumbling a crabby "no, thanks" before shutting the door firmly in my face. Finally, I would dip into my own meager savings or scrounge change from Dad's dresser—anything rather than bring back unsold stickers to the terrifying Sister Selsa Anne, or "Sarge," as us sixth graders called her. That was an embarrassment too awful to contemplate!

So, of course I helped my girls sell cookies, even though they practically sell themselves.

In fact, most people seem to wait expectantly for the season to roll around. Some even rub their hands together greedily while perusing the latest order form. And that is really the key to cookie success: to note which member of a particular family is most likely to buy not one, two or three boxes, but entire cases. That's when you know you've hit the mother lode!

Teenage boys and girls are easy. They're always hungry, but their wallets are often empty.

Moms always have plenty of buying power, but sometimes they're dieting and don't want the temptation.

Some fathers, on the other hand, just don't care about sweets, and so they order a box or two just to be polite.

The trick then, is to calculate which customers have all of these attributes: an enormous appetite, plenty of disposable income, absolutely no guilt about eating huge amounts of sugar, and a patriotic and thorough endorsement of Scouting in general, someone who ranks Girl Scout cookies right up there with Mom and apple pie.

That's the name you want to keep in your Blackberry for next year, unless you're like me—an old, veteran sales rep, now permanently retired.

Science Project Scares Parents
February 11, 2007

Rifling through a stack of papers piled up on my kitchen counter, I came across one at the very bottom that sent a cold chill down my spine.

"Science Fair Project Rubric," I read aloud and groaned.

Few things provoke as much anxiety and terror at our house as the annual commencement of the science fair. Apparently we're not alone in our frustration over science projects.

"Good lord, I have to get home and work on my science fair project," I overheard one father grumbling to a friend at a basketball game recently.

I chuckled over the realization that while kids moan and groan about science fairs, it's really the parents who bear the brunt of the misery.

My lack of interest, nay, loathing of science can be carbon-dated to the exact time of my very first science project.

I have no idea what experiment I performed, although I do have a dim recollection involving homemade toothpaste. I know for sure, however, that thereafter I suffered through the entire experience year after year, all through grade school.

My parents were far too busy to offer any guidance whatsoever, so I was totally on my own. Needless to say, the resulting efforts were never too impressive. In fact, the only thing I really remember from all those projects is that science can cause unimaginable stress, anxiety, frustration, and even terror.

No wonder then that I majored in liberal arts in college, avoiding any and all science classes as if they were the plague.

I know it is politically incorrect to admit this, but frankly my abhorrence of science continues to this day. That's why I always try to pawn these projects off on my husband.

"Science is your territory," I always tell him, but he usually rebels, even though he really does like science. We then argue about who needs to be in charge of nudging and eventually scolding our children into completing the task at hand.

Meanwhile, we all procrastinate even while we watch in horror as the due date circled on the calendar draws ever closer. Finally, a day or two before the project is due we all spring into action.

Out comes the handy book: "730 Easy Science Experiments with Everyday Materials." We flip through all the pages to find the most interesting (and easiest) one, then spend a small fortune on special display boards, new markers, alphabet stencils and glue.

Can all that really cost $75? After a frenetic 48 hours marked by much screaming, shouting and moaning, the project achieves some semblance of completion.

Invariably the last step is a special trip to school to help carry the behemoth into the classroom.

Once the experiment is safely out of my house, I always breathe a big sigh of relief. It's over with for another year. And next year I vow to be better prepared, to start earlier, and to cultivate a better attitude. Yeah, right!

Actually I'm always quite proud if my kids' science fair projects look somewhat pathetic because that's really what the outcome should be if a fifth-, sixth-, or seventh-grader actually performs the work.

The ones that are picture perfect and look as if they could have been created by Albert Einstein are the ones I always eye with suspicion.

Really, are you sure your fourth-grader created that exact replica of a human arm, complete with tendons that move each finger?

Did your fifth-grader actually study the effects of radiation sickness on that live lab rat?

Puhleeeease!

Probably I'm just jealous. Even with a lot of help from me, my kids' projects would still look like something a preschooler turned in. Of course, that lets me off the hook; they're definitely better off without my negative input and grumbling.

"I hope we don't win," my daughter recently exclaimed while working on her own science project, after hearing from peers about how dull the upper level competitions are.

I have to bite my tongue. Honey, I don't think you need to worry about that.

Good Husband Is Best Valentine
February 18, 2007

Holidays created to spur retail sales, like Valentine's Day, are bogus! I'm much too pragmatic to think that someone loves me just because they hand me a big box of chocolates one day a year or send me flowers that I have to pay for out of my household budget when the bill comes due.

I prefer a year-round romance, full of small, seemingly insignificant, everyday gestures that add up to one great big, long-term love affair.

Instead of chocolate, I love the delicious scent of coffee brewing in the morning as I sleep in an extra half hour while my husband takes over the early morning wake-up shift on school days.

I love getting into a car that's already been started and pulled up next to the front porch and not having to feed the cat or unload the dishwasher or fill the bird feeder.

I love when the phone rings in the middle of the morning because my husband is just "checking in" to tell me he loves me.

I love that he never complains about purchases I make, and in return I try (sometimes) to be frugal and financially responsible. He really can't complain on this topic, however, because he has tons more clothes than I do—a polo shirt or two and a hat for every golf course he's ever played, and there have been many.

I love that he is unbelievably patient with our children. When they were little I would try and hurry them out the door. "Come on, come on, come on, hurry up, hurry up, we'll be late," I would bark impatiently, in stark contrast to my husband's reaction whenever he was in charge.

"It's okay, we're fine, just take your time," he would croon, and everyone in the house would visibly relax.

Certainly, I wish he would routinely clean the garage and the shed, but if I can't have that, then I choose to be delighted by all the time he spends in the yard with his children, kicking the soccer ball, squatting behind home plate to catch strikes and shooting hoops in all seasons.

When our children were much younger they would all disappear into the woods for hours on end, traipsing along the path while their father regaled them with stories about animal tracks and deer trails and magical trees and jungle gyms created from uprooted oaks.

I love that my husband can make me belly laugh like no one else, that he loves to watch all the sporting events on television, but doesn't feel like he has to watch them all.

I love that he has coached all the sports our girls have participated in, even the ones he knows nothing about, and that he chose not to yell and scream at the kids but to compliment them and encourage them instead.

I love that he keeps the woodpile stacked on the porch and the fire stoked in the hearth, that he sometimes wakes me up on Sunday morning with a cup of tea made just how I like it, and that he insists on giving generously to the church because his father always told him, "It comes back to you many times over."

I love that he's smart enough to help the girls with their advanced math assignments, to figure out how to work the remote control, and to enjoy nonfiction books by Stephen Hawking and Stephen Ambrose.

I especially love that he treats everyone, whether a waitress or a bank president, a janitor or a state senator with the utmost courtesy and respect.

"When are you going to write about me?" he occasionally chides me.

Well, here it is honey, a belated valentine to you and the millions of men just like you out there—fathers, husbands, stepdads, brothers, uncles and boyfriends—who know instinctively that showing up, spending time, and giving your loved ones attention, respect, courtesy and affection, not just one day a year, but every day for many years, is the ultimate valentine, one that trumps Belgian chocolates and exotic hothouse flowers every single time.

5

Always kiss me goodnight.

— *posted in Fischer home*

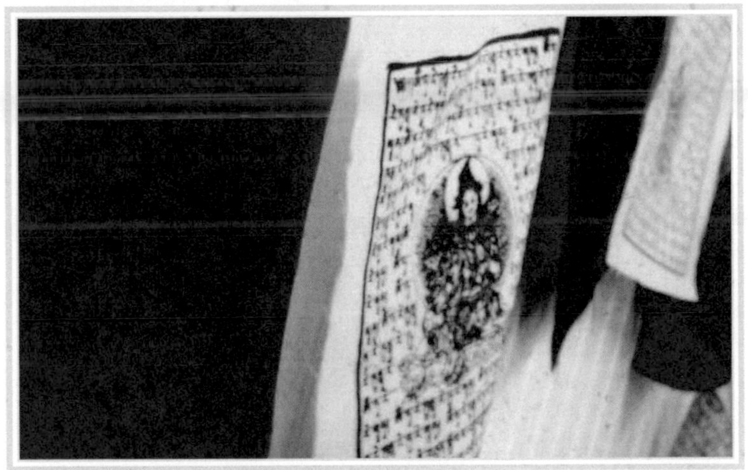

Mar 1, 2007 11:26 am

In case you haven't heard, we had a fire at our house February 20 while Joe and I were in Durham for our regular trip to Duke. No one was hurt and we're incredibly grateful for that. My sister and her daughter who were in Sedalia staying with the kids, and several workmen who were building our addition at the time, escaped the house before the fire got out of control. Thankfully, the girls were at school at the time. Unfortunately, the house was a total loss; it literally burned to the ground, although the garage and our vehicles were saved.

But we are not going to dwell on that and, of course, we're insured.

Joe's mother put us up until this past Tuesday when we moved into our temporary home: a magnificent, vintage, three-story stone house on Broadway.

The Broadway house is fabulous, roomy, a little antiquated and, according to several siblings who came down from St. Louis to help us move in and decorate, has several touches reminiscent of the brick home where we grew up.

Thanks to some hectic planning and ordering of necessities and an outpouring of generosity and help from both our families and so many friends, we are quickly moving toward normalcy.

And Joe, the strongest man I have ever known, already has reconstruction of our home moving at a rapid pace, with removal of the burned debris and the concrete foundation, which sustained too much damage to keep, all but done. I don't know when we'll be able to move back in but with Joe's efforts I know it will be sooner than anyone expects.

Again, I can't stress enough how the support here in Sedalia and from family and friends everywhere has shown how blessed we are to have that kind of a supportive network.

But what we really need now are photographs and other similar memorabilia and keepsakes that will help us preserve our memories of the past.

So, if you've got any photos of our family, please send us a copy, especially, of course, if any of our kids are in them. We remember what they look like but it's fun to have them in frames around the house, or in photo albums to pore over with a glass of wine during rainy and cold evenings when everyone else is out of the house.

We had to leave Duke early this trip because of the fire, but we go back next month and I'll give you an update after that trip.

I just felt it was necessary to say something because as people are finding out about the fire, they are trying to reach us. It is difficult to respond right now, and our internet connection won't be back for a few days.

We're fine. We love all of you very much.

1,000 Pictures Worth Words
Eighteen Months Earlier

Thank goodness our daughter's new soccer photos were available after the games Saturday morning. Since our last team picture was way back in June, during the softball season, an entire three months ago, we needed an updated picture to continue the documentation of her life's achievements.

Who cares that it will end up in an endless pile along with the many other sport and school photographs? In the end, it will be her problem to figure out what to do with all of them.

But that may become a significant problem if we continue on in this vein.

At the age of 8, she has more professional photos than I've had in my entire life. Surely this is the most photographed generation in America.

The only professional pictures I have from my childhood are a few school pictures showing me with goofy hairdos and even goofier grins, crooked teeth and all.

"Where are all the pictures of me as a baby?" I asked my mother when I was 9 or 10.

Already I had noticed that while my older siblings had adorable studio portraits hanging in the upstairs hallway, all of them in black and white, retouched and kindly blurred to enhance those sweet dimples and bright eyes, I was conspicuously absent from this family display, as were my younger siblings. Obviously the money for such things had run out about the time of my entrance into the world.

After being accused several times of this alarming neglect by her precocious seventh born, my mother finally handed me a torn, frayed photo one day, a photo of an ugly, scowling baby, with a mop of scraggly hair on top of her (or his?) head.

"This is you," she said when she handed it to me. "Yes, I'm sure this is you," she emphatically proclaimed, meaning, in other words, that she was not at all certain it really was me. I'm not sure she even knew if that baby belonged to the same generation as me.

Instinctively, I turned it over, looking for a mark or any information that could verify the identity of the baby in the photo. It was completely devoid of any writing whatsoever.

Very suspicious, I thought, since my dad was obsessive about marking names and dates on any and all photos, papers, books or documents that came into our home.

Still, it was obvious this was the best picture I was going to get, and so I kept it and enjoyed looking at it periodically, albeit with great skepticism.

What a different situation our children experience.

In addition to the long progression of sports pictures, my daughters have two pictures taken at school every year. When did school pictures become a twice yearly event?

It all seems a little redundant. If kids have goofy grins and crooked teeth in the fall, chances are they're going to look equally goofy in the spring picture. But parents, of course, will have to buy them both.

At a soccer tournament last year I noticed another interesting trend. A photographer was there taking "action" shots of the players on the field and making those same photos available online for parents to purchase. I found myself amazed at the thought of possessing such great shots of my daughter in action, shots that would document all her skill and prowess.

Surely there's a way to use such props on college entrance applications? I was just reaching for my checkbook when common sense intervened, for once. After all, how many photos of one young child does a family really need?

Of course, if you ask my children that question, the answer is simple. Their philosophy goes something like this: "If there is a picture of me anywhere out there in the universe and it's for sale, then we simply have to purchase it."

Still, I think even they are becoming immune to the allure of their image captured on acid-free paper. Whereas we used to argue about why we weren't getting the more expensive packages of photos—the ones with personalized buttons or faux magazine covers or (heaven help us) coffee mugs—by now they know the routine. We always buy the cheapest package available.

Even so, we've got more photos than we know what to do with. Alas, even Grandma and their many aunts and uncles have reached the saturation point. So, for now, the pictures will remain stashed in their memory boxes.

But as I continue to shove more photos into the already crammed boxes, I can't help but hope that this generation doesn't become too full of themselves. After all, to actually earn such unprecedented documentation, you really should accomplish more than just showing up for picture day.

Thank Goodness For Salt of the Earth
Mar 11, 2007

I could hear the muffled, collective groan all the way from Durham, North Carolina.

"Good grief! I have to cook for Susan Fischer again? She's so finicky about what she eats!" How taxing we have become lately on the sympathies and energies of our friends, family members and neighbors.

I literally wailed and thrashed around on the floor of our hotel room upon hearing the news that our house had burned to the ground.

It took at least an hour before the litany began in my head: My girls are safe, my girls are safe, my girls are safe!

Luckily we were forced to spend the night in Durham and thereby vented all our tears and rage and frustration over a half bottle of merlot in a cheap hotel next to the airport. When we finally arrived home to greet our children, we were able to speak calmly about how to proceed.

"We'll rebuild and replace everything," my stalwart husband quickly assured us.

But the only things I really care about are the very things that can never be replaced: dozens of DVDs documenting my babies' first steps, first words, first birthday parties, Christmases and Easters and Halloween parties and frolicking in the sprinkler in the front yard; scads of family photographs; original artwork by my uncle and godfather; my mother's cut-glass antique water goblets and her old walnut dining room table; a hand-crocheted coverlet made by my paternal grandmother; caricatures of my girls painted while on a family vacation; hundreds of beautiful books and my collection of original black-and-white etched prints.

In grim anticipation I am starting to hate the word new, knowing that soon everything I own will be new.

As a child the word conjured up all that was luxurious and superior. As an adult it seems limp and pale compared to the beauty and substance of the objects I have spent my lifetime collecting, like the funky Eames-like chairs I purchased at a roadside sale for $2 each. The back and seats were upholstered in an intoxicating bubble-gum-pink vinyl; the gorgeous mahogany wood swooped in sharply like an hourglass with only the slimmest piece connecting the chair's back to its seat.

I've seen my exact chairs pictured in several trendy home magazines and advertising layouts, so I know they were valuable. I may very well stumble upon something just like them in the future, but they won't have the aroma of that happy memory, the serendipity of finding a treasure for less than the price of a cup of coffee.

I'll also miss the 1940s table and the floor lamp I found with my brother-in-law while antiquing in Kansas City several years ago, and my potting cupboard, lovingly made by some rustic woodworker. It seemed made to order for the space on my front porch.

The simple pedestal library table where I used to sit and write my columns can be replaced, I guess. But it won't be the same one I've grown accustomed to over the years.

And I'll never own anything even remotely resembling the gorgeous handmade cherry bookshelf my best friend lavishly commissioned for me when we were restaurateurs together at age 25 and didn't have two cents between us.

Because I hate clutter, I constantly cull things from my house that I don't love. But these pieces I will desperately miss. I've been hauling them around from place to place for 20 years or more. And now they are all gone, up in smoke.

At least my trees will still be there, the Japanese maple planted when my mother died, the Japanese cedar purchased on clearance just before the Greenspot closed up shop, the river birch planted when my father-in-law died, and all the glorious trees in our woods, laden with wild honeysuckle.

Their beauty will be offset by the lovely old stones in our garden, huge slabs of old curbing, hand-hewn and laid lovingly to rest along our garden path.

New is great for many things, but when it comes to creating a life, a family, a home, I will always prefer the patina, the luster, the heft of old things, imbued with the collective memory of the human spirit.

Table of Plenty
House Beautiful magazine
Two Years Earlier

An exotic old dining table comes to symbolize the joys of everyday life in a large and loving family

It took four men to carry the table into the dining room, its walnut surface gleaming and as yet unblemished, at least to my six-year-old eyes.

"Damn it, Mary," my father grumbled. "This thing weighs a ton!"

As usual, he had almost no appreciation for the old furniture my mother periodically dragged home, and he utterly failed to recognize that this one was something special. But I noticed. Even at the ripe age of six, I loved the table.

To this day, I'm not sure how my mother cajoled him into buying it. With ten children in the house, food and clothing always took precedence over furniture, and my mother became adept at purchasing pieces from garage sales and junk stores. I always marveled at how the shaggy items she plucked from neighborhood sales (and sometimes trash heaps!) turned into tasteful, charming pieces once they were displayed in our living room.

But this was different. Even to my young eyes, this table was far more exotic than anything else in our house. The only exceptions were the items my mother had begun accumulating before her marriage but quickly gave up collecting as baby after baby arrived.

This splendid antique table, however, was destined to become the center of our home, of our very existence, and so its beauty became an integral part of our surroundings even though the surface eventually became scratched and marred, and parts of the veneer chipped away in large patches.

On that day, though, it seemed perfect: long and unusually wide, with beautiful carved lines decorating the side panels which surrounded the top surface, and three perfect arches, also beautifully carved, connecting two wide planks which supported the table top at either end.

The chairs that came with the table were equally stunning. Long before Parsons chairs were in vogue, my mother carried these into our dining room. Tall and stately with ornately carved walnut legs, the seats and backs were covered in a pale beige damask with only the faintest hint of peach. The fabric was stained and torn, in some places even hanging in shreds, but their regality called out to all that was romantic and sentimental in my soul. I just knew those chairs had come from some forgotten old castle or a palace from far away.

But alas, the chairs were relegated to the basement, their current shabby condition rendering them unacceptable even in our somewhat impoverished home, the idea of spending money to reupholster them being out of the question. Instead, the table was surrounded by newer chairs, maple in color, nondescript, but strong and functional.

I never learned where that table came from, whether it had once adorned the dining room of some wealthy family. Whatever its roots, however, it was in for much harder work amidst our sprawling family. Never a day went by that the table wasn't in almost constant use.

Every morning our school lunches would be lined up on it, wrapped in brown paper bags, each with our names scribbled hastily with the nub of some worn pencil.

Bologna or peanut butter and jelly on white bread were a certainty, occasionally accompanied by a bag of chips or a Little Debbie cake my mother had managed to hide from the ravenous horde of kids searching the kitchen after school for more and more and more to eat.

We knew all of her hiding places. Consequently, any treat purchased during Saturday's shopping trip and stashed for school lunches invariably disappeared long before Monday morning. We were insatiable, but paid for gorging ourselves on forbidden fruit with meager lunches throughout the week.

On our birthdays we would wake excitedly and run down to the dining room, where our presents would be spread out alluringly on the table.

They were never wrapped, a fact I didn't even notice until I was grown, when I realized that Mom's budget, for both money and time, was far too slim to afford a luxury like wrapping paper.

Here, too, we spread out the floral fabrics we painstakingly picked out to form our new Easter and homecoming dresses. Mom did most of the work, but always made us feel as if we had helped, indeed, as if we had done most of the work ourselves.

We were so proud to wear those dresses for the first time on Easter Sunday. We didn't often have new clothes. With eight girls in the house, hand-me-downs were plentiful, but Easter was always the exception. For Easter, we always had something new.

Around the table we spread out our homework nightly, side by side with my father, meticulously filling out his tax returns, or poring over blueprints of the buildings he was helping to erect.

We also ate all of our dinners there, for the kitchen of our two-story brick home, built around the turn of the century, was typically small. It contained a small table with a few chairs, but nothing large enough to fit us all. And every night we sat down together to eat an evening meal.

As we grew older, some of us would be missing, off at college, working or eventually married and out of the house. But the rest of us would gather to eat the meat and potatoes and canned green beans my father insisted upon, later to sample the parallel fare my mother favored—pasta with vegetables, zucchini and squash sautéed in butter and tomato sauce, cannelloni stuffed with spinach and multiple cheeses.

Often she would cook the equivalent of two meals, meatloaf and mashed potatoes for my father, and pasta and vegetables to satisfy her own palate. We, of course, inhaled it all.

Beginning when my older siblings first entered adolescence, dinners would almost always be followed by intense and often raucous discussions on everything from education to politics to religion.

It was the 1960s; my older brother and sisters were listening to Neil Young, Bob Dylan, and The Doors, and so we younger kids listened to them, too. Our large urban high school had so many students that classes ran in shifts, and the halls were full of kids who experimented with drugs, liquor and cigarettes. My siblings moved easily among this crowd, with their long, scraggly hair, work shirts, and low-cut bell-bottom jeans.

Our discussions around the dinner table were yet another venue for questioning the values of our parents' generation, and they allowed us that. They listened and let us rant and rave with the arrogant, uninformed opinions only the very young can put forth without embarrassment.

Sometimes my father would lose his patience and his temper, and we would know to back off of our thinly veiled criticism of his world, one we did not yet claim as our own. But always they allowed us to speak, to argue, to belittle—to ultimately find our own voice.

On holidays the table looked especially beautiful, for then it was always covered by one of my mother's old snowy linen tablecloths, a remnant from her wedding trousseau, which she painstakingly bleached, laundered, starched and pressed, preserving the cloth's loveliness long past its normal lifespan.

Then out would come her fine china (what was left of it, much of it having been broken or cracked through use by tiny hands). As we grew older, we were even allowed to use the delicate etched glass water goblets, thin as the daintiest seashell.

For flowers my mother would gather some beauty from her overgrown garden. She had an enormous interest in everything that grew in it, but no time to cultivate any but the hardiest of blooms. And so she would gather stems of holly at Christmas, forsythia and bluebells at Easter, and wild violets for summer celebrations.

Long after all of us had grown and wandered off on our own, these family dinners and discussions continued around the old table. Instead of nightly, they became weekly events.

Every Sunday my mother would begin cooking mid-afternoon, never knowing how many were coming or whether she would have enough food. But she always did, and we all came whenever we could, usually with our spouses (sometimes without) but always with our children, for they were completely at home at Grandma's house. There they were never told not to eat in the living room or to mind their manners. It was a chance for all of us to reenergize, to laugh and to argue with those who knew us best and loved us anyway.

Meanwhile, during all of this time, the lovely chairs that had come with the table still sat in a dark corner of the basement. As the years had gone by with no further money to reupholster the chairs, my father had begun to grumble. With so many people in one house, space was always at a premium. Anything not being used was gone.

But my mother persisted and whenever I made my way down to the basement to iron a shirt or fetch something from the freezer, I was comforted knowing that one day those chairs would be restored to their rightful glory, if not in my mother's house, then in my own.

Then one day they were gone.

I was home from college and had gone down to do my laundry when I noticed their absence. "What happened to those chairs, Mom?" I asked when I found her in the kitchen. She was peeling potatoes at the kitchen sink and didn't turn around. But she knew exactly what I was talking about.

"Your dad kept bugging me to get rid of them, so I did."

"What did you do with them?" I asked quietly.

"I put them out for the spring trash collection."

A moment of silence, both of us deep in thought. And finally she turned toward me, a rueful, smug expression on her face.

"They weren't there five minutes before a woman in a truck came by and hauled them off."

And suddenly we both laughed, enjoying somehow the certain glee of that unknown woman who had found a treasure beyond compare in the most unlikely of places, just as we mourned the loss of one of the finest things my mother had ever owned.

And, after all, Dad was right.

Our treasures couldn't be buried in the basement. They lived upstairs, above ground, in the loving and warm relationships between us, in the reverence for the nonmaterial things our parents had taught us, the love of honesty, hard work, tolerance, and, above all, family.

My mother died suddenly one Labor Day weekend, leaving this world no doubt as she would have liked, suddenly and without a lot of fanfare. Just as we had done many years before, when my sister died in a car accident at the age of 21, we sat around the dining room table and laughed and cried as we chose music and readings for the funeral, and reminisced about all the happy, chaotic times we had enjoyed together.

Two years after my mother's death, my father, ill with Parkinson's, shaky and unsure but always kind and gentle, moved in with my sister.

I lived three hours away and so left much of the packing up of the house to my siblings, who quietly divided among themselves the things that most reminded them of our mother. Finally, I was able to get away from work and my young children to help with the process.

Ironically, the house had never looked better. My mother, who would have enjoyed more than anyone the fresh paint on the walls and the woodwork and the newly sanded and varnished wood floors, was never to enjoy their beauty.

I wandered around the near-empty house, wondering what I wanted to take; I didn't need reminding, but I wanted something imbued with her spirit, and miraculously, there it was.

One of the few things I really loved in that house, that glorious old table, now chipped and scratched and coated with layers of invisible grime, was still there. None of my other siblings had chosen the table. They had unconsciously left it for me, who wanted it most.

In the kitchen I also found the thin, etched goblets we had always used on holidays, and in the marble-topped chest where my mother had stored her linens I found the delicate, hand-worked lace tablecloth she had purchased in Italy a few years before.

She had giggled over the exorbitant amount she had paid for it, but told me she just couldn't resist its charms. She must have told that story only to me, or perhaps I was the only one to ask, for when I mentioned it to some of my sisters, they didn't know what I was talking about.

I realized then that we each had our own unique memories of our mother in addition to the ones we all shared. No doubt they, too, had shared special moments like this one with her, but together they had spoken of other topics, topics of which I was unaware.

Now the table sits in my kitchen. Typical of newer homes, the room is spacious and light and airy. It is certainly the hub of our home, and so it is fitting that the table should be there.

Here we eat our evening meals together when we're not running to soccer practice or a basketball game or Girl Scout meetings. My three beautiful daughters address their valentines here, color Easter eggs, sort their Halloween candy, and play the new games they get from Santa Claus every Christmas.

For very special occasions I set the table with the Italian cloth, and of late I have even begun to use the etched-glass goblets, now that my girls are getting old enough to handle them and to appreciate their grandeur.

When I first brought the table home a few years ago, I paid several hundred dollars to have a new walnut top put on, but by now it, too, is scratched and marred from the tiny hands that constantly play over its surface, proving, as my mother always knew, that happy children and a full heart provide the greatest beauty of all.

Pickup Trucks
March 2007

You gotta love big, strapping men who drive pickup trucks: hard-working, God-fearing, apple pie-eating, baseball-playing, football-watching, churchgoing, kid-coaching, baby-hugging, barbeque-grilling men.

The first time I went out to see the burned shell of my ruined home, I had been prepared for the worst and so I was surprisingly calm.

In fact, what I most noticed was the beauty and serenity of the spot we have been fortunate enough to call home. Without the house on the horizon, the glory of the surrounding woods took center stage, making me feel awe at our great fortune in living there. Of course we would rebuild in exactly the same spot!

When I revisited the site twenty-four hours later, however, I was an emotional wreck. The tears began to flow as I pulled into my driveway and saw all makes and models and colors of pickup trucks—and a couple of SUVs—lining the long drive.

Almost two dozen men (and a few women) had interrupted their busy schedules, taken time off from their jobs, their businesses, and their many responsibilities to help clear away the detritus of our lives. Covered in soot from head to toe and wearing face masks, they pawed through the dust and rubble looking for any remnants of our life, while my female neighbors prepared lunch for the work crew.

My brother-in-law said he had had many offers to help but had accepted only a limited number, thinking a small team would work more efficiently than scads of people. I was profoundly moved to see the faces belonging to each pickup truck, every one of them long accustomed to hard work and perseverance, to taking care of family, neighbors, community—the proverbial salt of the earth.

Together they worked long and hard all day, with only a quick stop for lunch and a celebratory beer at the end of it all.

In the end they did salvage some interesting things we were able to carry home to our rental house in town, which we are now calling our "summer home." (After all, those pesky mosquitoes in the country can be downright nasty come August!)

My favorite find was a set of four stones given to me by my sister, each with a single word inscribed upon them: hope, peace, joy, love. They also found some of my mother's jewelry and a hand-thrown pot made by a friend and several other keepsakes we are thrilled to have back. My husband was delighted to discover a charred box containing his painstakingly unearthed collection of arrow heads, still perfectly intact inside.

Just about everything else was too burned or melted to repair or keep.

Still, I think the exercise was healing for my husband. When he came home at the end of the day, completely filthy and utterly exhausted, he had a huge smile upon his face.

"Everyone worked so hard and so smart," he exclaimed. "Everyone knew exactly what they were doing. We got the entire site cleaned out!" And I could tell he was extremely pleased to have accomplished such a nasty task so quickly, with people he admires and likes so much.

Since that day, the job site has seen a steady stream of workers, most of whom arrive via truck. Some are paid, some are not, some are friends or family members, some are not, some are very highly skilled, some are not. Day after day they have worked long hours, sometimes past dark with quick breaks for water or soda or cigarettes.

And slowly the house is beginning to rise again against the horizon. Every time I stop by to check the construction progress, I feel comforted to see the driveway full of pickup trucks, because I know the men who drive them are steadily giving me back my house, my home, my life.

I also feel comforted knowing I live in a town full of such men and that I'm married to one—a man completely comfortable driving a pickup truck, working hard, and taking care of family, neighbors and community.

New Garden Is My Strength
March 25, 2007

Spring is the worst possible time to be banished from my garden. To my immense relief, there are some lovely blooms peeking out around my "summer home," a few forsythia along the fence row, a large stand of daylilies just greening up against the garage, purple vinca peeking up from among the ivy branches, and several clusters of daffodils ready to pop open any day now.

Luckily, my sister brought me some gardening gloves as soon as I moved in here, because I'm anxious to dig in and start working, clearing off debris and leaves, trimming stray branches, uncovering ivy along the patio.

It doesn't matter to me that we will probably only live here for the summer. I will still derive great satisfaction from tending these plants, knowing that our summer home may be slightly better off because of our family's brief tenure here.

Of course, my garden this year will consist mostly of potted plants, but we have a lovely old, moss-covered-brick patio to display them upon.

When we first moved in, a relative offered to help me "get rid" of the moss covering the old bricks, but that's exactly the kind of old-world charm I would pay out the ear to reproduce at my new home. But alas, that's the kind of beauty you can't cheat on—only time and Mother Nature can create it.

Of all the spring blossoms, the forsythia is my favorite. My mother loved those best, too, probably because they grew so easily and bloomed profusely in her untended garden, but also because their bright yellow is one of the first harbingers of spring and always readily available for Easter centerpieces.

I miss watching my own forsythia every day, especially because I have four or five shrubs that I have been nudging along for a few years now, all to no avail. My efforts have yet to be rewarded with a big bloom.

A couple of seasons ago I transplanted several cuttings from a gigantic mama plant that took over an entire bed and, therefore, had to be cut out to make room for a new landscape plan.

I didn't realize that forsythia shrubs can quadruple in size so quickly. Each graceful stem bending gently down toward the earth springs into another plant when it touches the ground and thus divides into another and another and another enormous shrub. As usual, I should have listened to my older sister.

"Oh, that's a big mistake," she barked while visiting a few years ago and noticing my newly planted forsythia close to the house. "That thing is going to completely take over this area."

Of course, she was absolutely right, but that certainly wasn't the first and won't be the last gardening mistake I make since I prefer to learn in the field.

As my wise sister predicted, the mama shrub is long gone—requiring a Bobcat to remove all of the roots—but I've been nurturing several of her daughters for a few years (far, far away from my more formal flower beds), expecting that each year will produce the ultimate show of sunny blooms. So far, nothing! I'm afraid this will be the year, while I'm temporarily exiled from my garden, they'll finally come through with the goods.

I was quite surprised to note that the small, nondescript, gnarly shrub off the south side of the patio in my summer home has a few yellow forsythia blooms on it. Obviously, it needs some intense mothering to nourish it back to its more typical large, imposing radiant health.

And it is rather exciting to explore a new garden and wait patiently for each mysterious plant to reveal itself!

Surely those are spireas on our eastern border? But only the leaves and, ultimately, the blooms will tell us for sure.

I wonder what color the iris will be clustered in the southeast corner of the front yard?

And will all the daylilies be the same variety and color, or have they been intermixed for a dramatic, eclectic show?

I may have to sneak a cutting or two back to my permanent home if the colors turn out to be some I've been hungry for. Meanwhile, I'm patiently waiting—and watching.

Old Jeans Habit Hard to Break
April 1, 2007

With just a handful of items hanging in my closet these days, it is painfully apparent that, like most Americans, I only wear a fraction of what I own, even now, when what I own is only a fraction of what I used to wear.

There are obvious advantages to this: laundry is quickly done, not much time is lost agonizing over what to wear, and small closets are never a problem. However, I frequently have to chastise myself for wearing something too many times in a row.

The conversation in my head some mornings goes like this: You've worn your favorite jeans (luckily they survived the fire) for about three days straight. You really need to wash them—now.

But occasionally my alter ego slips up, too, and I'll find myself staring during the day at a stain on the leg of my jeans or the sleeve of my favorite (and only) cotton jacket.

Now how the heck did that get on there, I wonder, quickly followed by, how long has that been on there, and what exactly is that anyway? Spaghetti sauce? But I haven't had spaghetti since...

Well, you get the picture.

My husband also has occasionally swiped at my shoulder or arm with a wetted finger trying to dislodge and brush away some dust or lint or a smudge of food.

I've ordered plenty of new clothes, but they all seem to stay on the hangers. Even the perfect pair of black cropped pants I recently ordered for summer can't take the place of my favorite jeans. I'm almost afraid to begin wearing my "new" favorite pants, for fear that I'll wear them out quickly from constant use. It's almost as if I'm saving them for a really special occasion, just like our grandmothers would stash their fine linens and thus pass them on perfectly intact to the next generation.

Never mind that I've already ordered and accepted delivery on the perfect shoes and shirt to wear with the perfect new pants; somehow they are not yet tried and true.

They haven't yet passed the test of withstanding an entire day at the volleyball tournament or the school field trip without pinching or sagging or snagging or disappointing in some other way not yet imagined. Meanwhile, the receipt has been filed and stored just in case the perfect pants don't pass muster and have to be returned to sender.

Despite my reluctance to tear the tags off my new clothes, however, I have rapidly accumulated a sizeable pile of shoes.

They have all been worn and worn and worn, but I haven't yet stumbled upon that one perfect pair of black sandals that will carry me all through spring, summer and into fall. They'll have to be very versatile, able to go to the beach or the party with equal aplomb. Once I find them, they'll be on my feet constantly—with my perfect new pants, of course.

It usually takes the brusqueness of a sister to snap me out of a clothing obsession.

"I can't believe you are still wearing that old thing," an older sister remarked one summer after seeing me countless times in the same sundress. "I am sick of seeing that thing," she wailed.

Of course, it was on its way down to the Open Door just a few days later.

Thank goodness friends and acquaintances are more polite and civil than sisters. On the other hand, if friends were more abrupt, perhaps we'd clean out our closets more often. We'd certainly end up with fewer clothes, but I guess we'd have fewer friends as well.

"Honey, those jeans may be your favorites, but they are no friend to your backside."

Such honesty might save us all from misguided clothing obsessions. But then, the friendship might not survive for long.

I guess in the long run I prefer civility to brutal honesty. So, if you see me wearing the same old thing day in and day out, perhaps with a little spaghetti sauce sprinkled on it somewhere, cut me some slack—I really don't have anything else to wear, at least until I break in my new favorite stuff.

Spring 2007

A small miracle unfolds in my dining room each evening these days, the first of many to unfold I am sure for my family in this coming year of rebuilding and healing.

My in-laws delivered to us a lovely antique dining room set to use in our summer home. We were delighted to have a lovely old large table to once again stack our piles of research materials upon and together gather around at the end of an exhausting day.

But the real miracle is that through some divine shift in the universe, a realigning of the stars and the end of the ball season, we are all home together almost every evening for dinner.

And just as our mouths begin to water and our stomachs to rumble, the door opens and some kind soul delivers to us a delicious, home-cooked gourmet meal, ready to set upon the table. I have been completely humbled and moved every evening to tears by everyone's slavish attention to my culinary whims!

Every meal has included some delicious wholesome protein, crucial for balancing my blood sugar and helping me through chemotherapy along with multiple varieties of rainbow-colored vegetables and fruits. We've had my favorite vegetable, asparagus (one that rarely has high pesticide residues, according to my nutritionist), in more delightful ways than I can count. As we plan our walled kitchen garden at the new house, I insist that asparagus will be the first crop to go in!

This hearty food cooked for us by so many kind souls in Sedalia has nurtured our hearts, our bodies, our minds and our souls.

As I look over the list of amazing women who have volunteered to cook for us I am touched and honored at the number of strong, intelligent, creative, amazing women I have the honor of calling friend. I must be doing something right to have attracted all of you into my life!

We will always remember that you have wrapped your strong, nurturing, loving, cooking arms around our family during one of our darkest and most perplexing moments.

If my healing miracle is to occur this year, and I feel that it will occur, it will be in large part because you have literally given me back my strength and my fighting spirit.

I am determined to grow old and curmudgeonly in the midst of such graceful and witty company. I'm also determined that no bitch but me will tend my walled English garden, now that I've cajoled Joe into building one for me!

After leaving the hospital feeling somewhat like a concentration camp victim, gaunt and skeletal, I now have steroid-fat chipmunk cheeks and a rounded tummy again, thanks to all of your delicious food.

I also have a cabinet full of new casserole pans, pots, fun picnic supplies, Tupperware, etc., one totally "bitchin" basket, and a renewed appreciation for the power of women to conquer all obstacles!

My sisters, mother-in-law and brother-in-law have partaken of your wonderful repasts as well. Kind of like the fishes and the loaves, there always seems to be plenty for whomever is around! My sister from St. Louis lost five pounds while here by eating so healthy. God bless each and every one of you.

One evening after we had just consumed a delightful picnic on our patio delivered by the very creative Lynn and Mike

Robinson, my daughter exclaimed: "I love that we still live like we're in the country even though we live in the city."

I just wanted all of you amazing women out there to know that every evening as we bow our heads and pray before partaking of the nourishment you've provided, our first blessing is for the many friends who have come to our rescue yet again.

We love you all,

Susan

Summer Romance Is the Best
Spring 2007

This new adventure was supposed to be only a summer fling. We would walk away after a few months with no attachments and no hurt feelings. The flaw in the plan, however, is that I am falling madly in love with the quiet beauty and romance of my summer home.

Sure, I miss my modern faucets, where the hot and cold water actually merge into a steady temperate stream, instead of boiling hot on the left and freezing cold on the right and "never the twain shall meet."

I also miss my huge laundry room and modern showers. (Note the use of the plural—as in, more than one!)

But as I gaze around the near empty rooms of this gorgeous Victorian mansion, I feel such a romantic interest in the people who commissioned and built and lived in this beautiful home, now 103 years old.

I look with fascination and awe at the craftsmanship all around me and wonder if my new house will still be beautiful when it is 100 years old, or will it even survive for 100 years?

I grew up in an old house and always thought I would live in one as an adult. As much as I loved my home in the woods, I often daydreamed about renovating an old mansion, just like the one we're in now.

I've always been a sucker for big tall ceilings, and beefy crown molding makes my knees weak. I'm crazy for old, wavy original handblown-glass panes, especially when they're presented in a mullion casement window with no less than three dozen separate panes of glass, all set on the angle of a diamond. I swoon into a hot bath in our antique footed-bathtub and gaze lovingly at the oval pedestal sink, probably original to the house. The wallpaper is old and faded, peeling in places, but it completes the scene, the sense of having taken a giant leap back in time, and most of the rooms have built-in drawers and cabinets that are elaborate and quirky at the same time.

I also love the idea of the third floor, probably the servants' quarters judging by the stairs, which suddenly get steeper, and the wood flooring, which gets rougher and less exotic. Still the sitting room up there is simply flooded with light flowing in from the intricate mullion windows, and the bedrooms have built in drawers and closets.

I can just imagine the hustle and bustle early in the mornings as the worker bees rose early to provide breakfast trays for the family members on the floor below. I do realize, however, that I probably would have been one of those worker bees.

My maternal grandmother, Helen, left the family farm in Pilot Knob, Missouri, at the age of 13 to be a "house girl" for some affluent family in St. Louis. Growing tired of deflecting advances from the man of the house, she soon left to work in a factory, probably harder work but safer in the long run, or so goes the family lore.

But today, the blooming branches of the redbud tree and the dogwoods present cheery bouquets to me every morning as I gaze out my bedroom window in our charming summer house. And during the last of the cold nights of winter, I tucked my youngest daughter into bed by the light of the gas fire on her bedroom hearth.

And who knew that walking in town with a purpose is so much fun? It's such an adventure now to walk to Sonic for a Slush or to a friend's house or just home from school. It beats the heck out of walking endlessly 'round and 'round and 'round the track just for exercise. To actually have a destination in mind when you set out gives just a hint of the kind of adventure Lewis and Clark must have felt a century before my sweetheart house was built.

I know that my new home will be much more comfortable than this one when it's done and equally beautiful. And my heart will be all aflutter when we move back into our old/new house, but my summer romance with this Victorian beauty will remain with me for life.

Apr 18, 2007 8:40 pm

Susan and Joe are at Duke where she will undergo an operation Thursday morning to relieve pressure on her brain from what is likely to be a combination of tumor regrowth and an accompanying cyst.

They are not alone in Raleigh. Joe's sister, Mary Ellen, and Susan's sister, Beth, are both there for moral and logistical support. Please send them all your prayers. We'll post more information when it is available.

Apr 19, 2007 5:13 pm

Dr. Sampson, Susan's surgeon, said the operation to de-bulk the tumor went well. He felt that they removed about 70% of the tumor regrowth. Susan is resting. As always, prayers are the best medicine we can dispense out here.

A Few Moments in My Corner
May 7, 2007

Just a few days before flying south to Duke University for another brain surgery, I finally got around to watching the film "Cinderella Man" while resting at my sister's home.

"Oh, you'll enjoy this film. It's pretty uplifting and inspirational," she said. Since my 13-year-old nephew was lobbying hard for "Benchwarmers," I, of course, chose Russell Crowe.

But after an hour of watching beleaguered pugilists pummel each other nearly senseless in slow motion while outside the ring their families and society in general fell apart under the terror and stress of the Great Depression, I couldn't for the life of me find any inspirational message there.

And yet, it seems like a great metaphor to describe how I feel as a cancer patient about to enter round two of my epic battle with this modern-day pestilence.

I have a brief moment in my corner to huddle with my coach and manager and loved ones, to garner their advice and support before being propelled out into the ring once again to battle my adversary—ready or not.

Meanwhile, my pulse is racing, my heart is beating, my eyes feel as if they're rolling around in my head—too much information again, too much advice: "Stay away from his left, hit him with your right."

Way too much Decadron making me feel something surely akin to the jitters of Parkinson's. A jolt of smelling salts to clear your head, a little salve on my cuts and bruises and once again I'm propelled into the ring to prevail or go down fighting.

I'm getting stronger every day after the trauma of this second surgery and I count my blessings daily for the skill of this second young surgeon who has saved my life. But I am a little exasperated that while our modern day physicians reach ever-more-giddy heights of knowledge, we also seem to be jettisoning important teachings from the ancients.

"Let food be your medicine!" proclaimed Hippocrates, the father of modern medicine.

Why then, can the Duke team drill through my skull and resect cancer without turning me into a vegetable, yet be unable to serve me one meal perfectly situated on the glycemic scale to prevent the surge in blood sugar caused by Decadron?

Why is it that they can completely stymie my pain for days on end without stifling my memory, but they cannot re-populate the friendly bacteria in my digestive tract, or clean out my colon enough to send me into the world feeling like a functioning person?

How much easier must these tasks be than the radical surgery they had performed?

I don't see much hope for conquering this beast that is cancer until the modern, brilliant, new remedies are paired with the ancient wisdoms.

I know the hospital staff members were shocked and perhaps a little mortified when we busted out of the hospital on Friday night, the evening after my surgery.

"Dr. Freidman always requires his patients to stay a week!" I heard one intern sputter.

Luckily, my renegade surgeon is much younger and counting on my strength and vigor to pull me through, so he released me and I was glad to go even though I was a little nervous about leaving the sterile confines of the Western model.

But I knew in my heart that while their skill and dedication and brilliance had saved me once again, my true healing would come about outside those walls, somewhere along the axis where Western medicine and the wisdom of the ancients connects, forming the union of perfect healing and perfect harmony, of mind and body and spirit.

And so I was wheeled down to the lobby of the hospital and out into the parking lot by a young immigrant man—two months fresh on American soil from Nigeria—who handled my chair with complete humility and dignity.

We spoke very little but I could see by the compassion on his face that he was full of kindness and good wishes.

As we broke out into the open air of daylight, I felt such a rush of gratitude to be alive and heading home to my family.

Now as I slowly recover I'm trying to wait patiently for life's inexorable tug to lift me once again and carry me along through another difficult year, bearing in mind Robert Frost's all-encompassing phrase about life: "It goes on!"

And so it will be for me. But for now, grant me just a few more moments in my corner before I begin getting the ever-living daylights beat out of me again.

Good grief, this doesn't mean I have to watch "Rocky V," does it?

Reluctantly, Susan Fischer has decided to take a sabbatical from her column while she devotes her time to rebuilding her health and her home. Her column may appear occasionally throughout the summer.

6

Take care of my girls...

May 25, 2007 4:35 pm

Greetings from down under! I am feeling better every day as the Decadron fog begins to lift.

Today is my first day of tapering! Thank God for my sisters and sister-in-law, who abandoned their husbands to be here to listen to me gnash my teeth, wail, and cry every five minutes. But I'm still being dubbed the Deca-dragon by my loved ones!

An unexpected balm to my heart and soul appeared last night shortly before yet another delicious nutritious meal arrived on our doorstep. I was spending a few moments in quiet meditation on my brand-new, very expensive chair designed just for that purpose. (I know, there's something patently ridiculous in how us baby-boomer yuppies spend so much time and energy in search of a Zen-like simplicity, but I am enjoying my new chair.)

And while I was sitting there focusing on its abundance, I received an unexpected phone call from my amazing nutritionist Jeanne Wallace in Utah. She said she couldn't "end her day without checkin' in on me."

She has more than 700 brain tumor patients, thirty of whom are currently doing really well on the Avastin protocol. In fact, only one has not responded to the Avastin, but she said his is a much more serious case than mine.

She thinks this is absolutely the right course of action and emphasized the importance of having 75% of that tumor now gone due to the last surgery, and said she is ready and willing to help me with nutritional support to offset any side effects that may crop up and with tapering off the Decadron and dealing with rebound inflammation, mood alterations, fatigue, adrenal exhaustion, etc.

I'm strong enough to handle this next round of treatments, probably for about a year without many side effects or complications, and we will gain a remission, which means the combination of my complementary and conventional therapies, along with my sheer stubbornness, can work my miracle.

I also plan to continue my vitamin C infusions as often as I can, preferably two per week, until that becomes too overwhelming.

Meanwhile, I'm not allowed to drive at least until I check back in with the surgeon at Duke in 4-6 weeks, so I appreciate everyone helping to run my kids around. And thank God I do not have to drag my butt off to the night shift every day to support my new prescription drug habit.

My new house is going to be more fabulous and gorgeous than we probably need or even deserve but Joe has pretty much given me carte blanche, and I am not one to turn down an opportunity like this!

I thank God every day that I have not one but two huge, amazing families to take care of me and love me!

I feel that I am healing every moment already!

Love you all,

Susan

Household Words to Live By
Two Years Earlier

I love the fact that words are back in fashion. They're everywhere—on plaques in all the home goods stores, on garden stakes, on pillows, on T-shirts. And I love them all.

"Don't bug me!" a plaque proclaims on my screened-in porch, where I often sit to read the newspaper in late afternoon or early evening when the weather cools off.

My guests frequently notice the sign and smile over its message. In fact, the only ones who don't notice the sign are my children, for whom it is intended. They simply ignore it, and continue to bug me almost constantly.

"Simplify" a sign in my dining room berates me. I know, I know, how ironic! If I were really simplifying, I wouldn't be shopping in the home furnishings store where I purchased the sign, and my home and garage and shed wouldn't be overflowing with more stuff—much of it pure junk—than one family can ever use.

Still, it's nice to keep a reminder around. Actually, since I need extra reminding, I bought two "simplify" signs, each of them unique, and now I have one on the front porch, too.

"It's All About Me" hangs on the wall in my daughter's room, and truer words have never been spoken.

"Queen of Everything" or "Princess" or "I Am Not Amused" would also apply to my three daughters' pampered lifestyle, but I haven't run across those signs in the appropriate colors yet. Or maybe I'm just being successful at simplifying!

"Always Kiss Me Good Night" is perched on a shelf in yet another bedroom. Sage advice for any family, this phrase sums up all my maternal instincts and the gush of love I feel for my daughters, whenever they're not bugging me, that is.

When they were much younger, my children would allow me to kiss their sweet foreheads and cheeks dozens of times in quick succession; I could never get enough of their innocence. As my daughters grow, however, the plaque becomes more of a reminder for them than for me. I don't think I can ever forget to kiss them goodnight. But all too soon I fear they will have outgrown the need for my kisses.

"Oo Lah Lah" screams out a small, black, silk pillow hanging in my teenager's bathroom, while "Dream" is carved out in glittery silver cardboard and hangs in her bedroom. Or at least it did until she decided that was too sappy a sentiment for a growing young woman. Just recently I moved the sign to my guest room, hoping it would inspire sound sleep for my siblings who visit periodically.

Our home isn't big enough to contain our many word plaques and so they spill out into the garden.

"Grow," a decorative plant stake implores the abundant

flowers surrounding it. And in my mind I silently apply the adage to my young family, wishing for them to grow strong and smart and old, wishing for them to outlive me by many years.

A stone half-buried next to my dwarf Alberta spruce is engraved with words from Robert Browning, "Grow Old Along with Me, the Best is Yet to Be," words which also adorned my wedding invitations many years ago.

I'm not sure we've reached the "best" part yet, unless that's defined by trying to soothe chickenpox bumps for three weeks straight with very little sleep, or listening to siblings yell and scream at each other all day long during the hot summer months, or spending endless hours in hot, stuffy gyms watching our children lose games or, worse yet, sit on the bench while their teammates lose games.

But I'm optimistic about the next decade and the empty nest thing!

My favorite sign is the most profound: "Be Still and Know That I Am," it silently sings to me, hanging next to my cluttered desk in the kitchen.

I sometimes do attempt to sit quietly and meditate, for I believe, as the Hindus do, that if you can truly quiet your mind, then you can hear the voice of God.

I believe the premise wholeheartedly, I just can't manage to put it into practice. After about ten seconds of quiet, my mind fills to the brim with what I need to accomplish that day or with ideas for another story, or just with how hard it is to actually empty my mind. Still, the sign is a welcome reminder of what is really important, a constant rejoinder to resist what the Bible calls the "witchery of paltry things."

I guess my many plaques, my fascination with everything written, could also be considered paltry, but for me the magic of words is anything but.

In fact, at my house, the poetry and magic of words are nothing short of sheer majesty.

May 31, 2007 1:53 pm

Chopra Center is great! La Costa resort gorgeous.

Joe and I are skipping 7 a.m. yoga to sleep in and breakfast together on our private terrace surrounded by birds of paradise, purple and white agapanthus and thousands of orange marigolds. The scent is intoxicating!

Then on to group meditation, lectures on "perfect health" and harnessing mind/body healing techniques and the ancient medicine of India, Ayurvedea, then daily massages, with lots of oils and more oils—we're a greasy mess!—steam rooms and saunas, more meditation, strolls through the grounds, great meals, lots of ginger tea and lots of relaxation. Just what we need!

I am feeling strong and keeping up although I do need to slow down occasionally. Tapered off again on Decadron on Wednesday, and still have about 7-8 weeks left, but the final ones will be tiny doses—can't wait!

Meanwhile, I have totally fat cheeks and belly and I am tired of eating all the time. Never thought I would say that!

We'll be home late Saturday night. Friends arrive from India via Colorado sometime on Sunday for a week. So I will have lots of loving and nurturing from them.

And Rachel has successfully joined her travel group in Italy—another miracle unfolded there. Thanks for everyone's help in pulling that off – getting the long-awaited passport, and transporting her to Kansas City to catch an alternate flight, in our absence.

Things do work out in the end, thanks to the infinite organizing ability of the abundant universe. It's just not always on my timetable according to my plan, which is what I'm working on out here. Detaching from the outcome!

Love,
Susan

Once a Soldier, Forever a Soldier
Two Years Earlier

I was out of town this Memorial Day weekend, so I was unable to hang a flag on my porch to honor American veterans, but the flag is waving this morning as I think about the many soldiers of this generation who are serving their country, and about the many soldiers of past generations, like my father, whose military service altered his life forever.

William Thomas O'Brien, or WTO as he came to be known, was many things throughout his long life: husband, father of ten children, carpenter, and an intelligent, compassionate man. But shortly after his nineteenth birthday, in 1942, he earned the title that would shape the rest of his life; he became a soldier.

WTO was one of the lucky ones to survive World War II and after two and a half years in the Army Air Force he became a veteran. But in his heart he was always a soldier. His character and subsequent life were shaped and molded by his experiences during the war.

Some of those experiences he remembered as happy ones (three squares a day), some comical and many tragic and deeply troubling to the earnest, intelligent, sensitive young man who shipped out overseas in 1943.

"I was only in the Army a short time, but I knew the gap between me and the world I left behind was miles and years apart," my father wrote many years later while chronicling his military experiences for his family.

Many years after the war, when my siblings and I were still very young, we would roll our eyes and moan as Dad attempted to interest us in yet another war story. We would joke among ourselves about how every topic someone brought up led inevitably to another military anecdote.

My husband first endeared himself to my father during our courtship because he could sit and listen to endless stories about my father's military career. I thought he was merely being polite and diplomatic. But many years later, now that we are married and have children of our own, I realize that he was listening intently.

When the conversation around the dinner table turns to my father, it is my husband and my brothers who know most about his military career and the details of his life in the Army Air Force.

Perhaps that is because during our teen years, when my sisters and I were interested in dating and parties, these young men knew that they, too, might be called upon to enter some battle, to offer up for their country and their loved ones the greatest sacrifice, putting one's life in harm's way.

Certainly many women serve their country in this way today, and many participate frequently in the heat of battle and endanger their lives by doing so. But compulsory service for women in our country has no history and, therefore, the majority of young women today cannot know the fear, the curiosity, the lure of war.

Yet in our patriarchal culture there can be no greater test of a man's courage and conviction than how he handles himself when called upon to support a worthy (or not so worthy) cause.

During these troubled times, with murmured talk of the insufficiency of our standing army, the topic must be in the minds of every parent whose sons and daughters are in their late teens.

"How would we react if called to serve in this particular war?"

My father had no such ambivalence about his own service. The call was clear back then. Our country had been attacked and we had to defend ourselves. My father enlisted in the Army Air Force, knowing that if he waited until he was called to serve, he would have far less choice about how and where he did so.

Initially, my father had hoped to train as a pilot, but because of color-blindness he worked as a mechanic and then as a top-gunner on the B-29, flying many missions in China, Burma and India, and earning the Distinguished Flying Cross and other medals.

How fitting, then, that when my father died in 1998, he was interred at Jefferson Barracks National Cemetery in St. Louis.

The funeral service remains one of the most poignant memories of my life: watching two young Marines snap and carefully, dexterously, fold the American flag with their white-gloved hands, while a lone bugler played "Taps" 100 yards off upon a slight hill, surrounded by headstones, all of uniform shape, size and spacing, placed with typical military precision.

And how ironic, too, that at his funeral, when it was too late to listen to his stories, I finally understood the enormity of his military service and how it had affected his entire life.

I finally realized that military service is only insignificant to those who have never been called upon to serve, or more importantly, know they never will be called upon to serve.

For my father's generation, military service—how a man answered the call in his country's time of need—defined who he was, and who he would become.

In short, it was everything.

Family Returned to Old Galway
Two Years Earlier

"My dear Julia," wrote my great-grandmother to her daughter (my grandmother) in 1921, upon hearing of her engagement in America. "You can imagine darling, how I feel. I always longed and hoped for your return to Ireland, but when you did not care to come, it was no use in pressing you. I will have one consolation, to know you'll have a good protector and home, then I'll have no need to worry. Your sister Mary will feel it very much (though), as she expected you home."

After nearly three years of planning and plotting and saving, my family experienced the trip of a lifetime and visited Ireland to meet our cousins, the offspring of my great-aunt Mary, who very much wanted her sister to come back to Ireland.

Two sisters, born in Ireland and raised in America, were separated when the elder sister's husband inherited the family farm back in County Galway.

"It must have been terrible for her here," my cousin recently mused about his grandmother and her return to Ireland after living in America.

We were sipping a pint in an ancient Dublin pub called McDaids, just off Grafton Street, full of beautiful, dark paneling, ornately carved woodwork and a massive mirror, clouded by time, hanging behind the bar—a perfect place to reminisce about family and country.

Since pubs in Ireland are family-friendly, my daughters were sitting there beside us, albeit slightly jet-lagged and wearing the same clothes in which they had crossed the Atlantic, because the airline had lost our luggage.

This is why we've come so far, I thought, to revel in this sense of place and family and history.

I had spent eight months with my cousins after graduating from university and they had visited America on several occasions, including the time they surprised me just before my wedding day. But I wanted my daughters to spend time with their Irish cousins and to get to know them well.

"That area around Galway was so remote then," my cousin continued as we discussed his grandmother Mary's life in Ireland over a Guinness. "She wouldn't even have been able to get coffee!"

No doubt, the woman was in serious need of some coffee. With nine children to take care of on a remote farm with very few conveniences, an extra shot of espresso in a caramel machiatto from Starbucks would have been just the ticket.

"Well, Julia dear," my great-aunt Mary wrote in another letter to her sister, dated May 1921. "I don't think I can ever feel happy here, although I have a very nice place, but I miss everything there in America so much and the country is in such an upset state."

In 1921, Ireland was in the midst of a civil war which must have made Mary feel even more alienated in the countryside around Galway.

"I suppose you hear a great deal about Ireland. I don't want to say much as I want you to get this, but whatever you hear is right, as it is terrible in some places. The torture and death of boys and men. One of our Galway priests was shot and found in a wood. All we can do is pray to God to protect us as everyone wants peace."

That lasting peace my great aunt prayed for finally may have come to Ireland this year. On the last day of our trip we picked up the newspaper to read over our morning tea and saw an astonishing headline: "A Farewell to Arms: The IRA Stands Down."

My daughters were full of questions as my husband and I began discussing what Tony Blair called "a step of unparalleled magnitude," and we answered to the best of our abilities, but we felt our ignorance keenly. Still, my daughters added a few more paltry facts to their growing store of knowledge about this beautiful country from whence we came.

My daughters are obviously too young to have any interest yet in the dozens of old letters between my grandmother and her family members in Ireland. But I'm determined to stay in touch with our Irish cousins because I have no doubt that one day, my daughters will come upon these letters and be intensely interested in them.

And when that happens, I want them to have a better sense of who these people were, what they felt and how they suffered. For in knowing them, they will certainly have a better understanding of the world, and perhaps a little more compassion for those who abide in it.

Should Mom Vote for Pope?
Two Years Earlier

"Did you vote for the pope, Mom?" my 7-year-old daughter asked me earlier this week, noticing the "I Voted" sticker on my shirt.

"No, honey, I didn't," I answered. "I was voting for school board candidates."

And that was hard enough, I thought to myself.

Later, as I waited in line at the bank, it occurred to me that voting for the pope isn't such a bad idea. In recent years, especially as Pope John Paul II grew increasingly frail, the Catholic Church has become somewhat out of touch with its one billion parishioners.

No, I'm not going to bash the Catholic Church. I was born and raised on its pomp and circumstance and I have grown to love the beauty and meaning of its rituals, despite the fact that I have not always been the best Catholic.

During my rebellious high school years, my sister and I would routinely skip our Confraternity of Christian Doctrine classes and drive around smoking cigarettes. I can't say we felt great about our delinquency, but the classes were resoundingly boring and we were desperate to strike out against the establishment.

In college I almost never went to Mass, although when visiting home, I would often get up early to attend Mass with my mother. She never asked me to go or made me feel guilty about not going, but I craved this time with her. Even in the midst of my great breach with the Church, her quiet, simple faith was leading me back to the fold.

My mother was a devout Catholic. Her faith brought her great comfort and strength during many difficult times in her life: the death of a 21-year-old daughter, the cancer and long-term illness of a teenage son, and the less urgent sorrows of raising ten children on two salaries that were never quite enough.

Through the gracious way she reached out to everyone around her, the way she lived the message of Jesus, my mother was able to instill in her children something of the beauty and the truth of the faith which served as her lifeline.

She conveyed that message most powerfully, however, not through dictating to us about it but by showing us an example of how much easier a life could be when infused with a power greater than any we possess on Earth. And even though she insisted we attend church, she also allowed us to question our faith. Her quiet example was a large part of what finally brought me back to the Church many years later.

These days, my husband and I usher our three daughters into morning Mass at St. Patrick's Church every Sunday, and I consider myself a good Catholic in progress. But thanks to my enlightened mother, I continue to question and debate Church doctrine.

So, not surprisingly, during the presidential election last fall, I was insulted by the arrogance of some Catholic priests who proclaimed that those who voted for anyone other than pro-life candidates were unworthy to take communion—because we are all unworthy to take communion!

In fact, we say those very words before we approach the altar. And as one priest replied when I questioned him on the topic, "There are many 'pro-life' issues besides abortion." Providing food, clothing, shelter and medical care for the poor, the disabled and the elderly are also "pro-life" issues. And keeping our environment clean and able to sustain life for our great-great-grandchildren is yet another "pro-life" issue.

I am also dismayed that the Church continues to ignore how many Catholics feel about birth control. I don't know any Catholics of this generation who have eight and ten children, and I'm quite certain it's not because they are all great at the rhythm method. Does that make all of us "bad" Catholics?

Before she passed away several years ago, my mother and I

had many conversations about this topic.

Even though she loved all of her children with her heart and soul, she knew firsthand how impossible it is for two parents to give the necessary time and energy to ten children.

She said that she felt powerless and unable to make her own choices in a time when all the men of her church—the priests, bishops, cardinals, and yes, the pope—were telling her that ten pregnancies and two miscarriages was the price she had to pay for being a "good" Catholic.

Meanwhile, some male priests were still considered "good" Catholics as they continually molested children. When accused, many were simply reassigned.

Furthermore, women still are not allowed to celebrate the Mass, even though the Church is experiencing a severe shortage of priests. Perhaps, at the very least, women should be allowed to serve as deacons, just as men are.

In my own way, I will continue to teach my children about the beauty and truth of the Catholic religion, which, after all, transcends the puny acts of mere mortals. But I will also encourage them to question their faith and to try and change those things about the Church with which they do not agree, just as my mother encouraged me to do.

I don't really want to vote for the pope. I'm not smart enough or good enough to make that call. But I do want the cardinals to think about me, one of the billion parishioners they speak for, when they make their decision on who will lead our Church through the next generation.

Jun 26, 2007 10:03 pm

We are having another great week away, this time in New York. How fun to finally be able to travel without a backpack and with more than $7 in your pocket at a time!

We are literally eating our way through the city, going from one fabulous meal to the next, lemon and ricotta pancakes, spinach and goat cheese omelets, salmon, tuna, rack of lamb, at all hours of the day and night.

Needless to say, these sumptuous repasts are not helping my Decadron-fattened belly! I look like I'm about four months pregnant.

I am down to only six mg per day now, though with only about 6-7 weeks longer to go on this nasty stuff, and we are walking quite a bit, so I'm actually beginning to feel some calf muscles emerging from my steroid-weakened muscles! Even though I've been moving very slowly throughout the city, with multiple stops to rest, the walking has been great for me and I've handled it better than I thought I might.

Joe has been great, as always, taking thorough care of me, and smoothly navigating the subway system and the city. He even procured us half-price tickets to "A Chorus Line" from the kiosk at Times Square.

We've also seen the Guggenheim and the Planetarium, strolled through Central Park, shopped at Room and Board and from various dubious street vendors, spent time with Joe's nephew and his wife, and toured the Village Voice.

I spent six hours of therapy with Dr. Bollentino and today we go to meet her mentor, Larry LeShaun. He is retired at 87 but spent 35 years researching and writing the book "Cancer As a Turning Point."

The book explains how patients who use their illness to redirect their lives, keeping what they're passionate about and jettisoning what isn't working, frequently survive their cancers and go on to live many years longer than other patients.

Makes perfect sense, of course, and perhaps we didn't need to come here to figure that out, but any excuse for a fun week with my honey is my new motto!

If nothing else, we confirmed what I already knew; I have the perfect life already! Amazing spouse, great kids, two big loving families, an entire community of friends who support and sustain me, and work that I'm passionate about, even if it doesn't pay much! Or, hakuna matata (no worries), as we heard in "The Lion King" yesterday.

Anyway, we arrive home Tuesday afternoon. We're doing great and I'm starting to feel more like myself.

We had the first ceremonial firing of the fireplace at the new house with the friend who designed it and it works wonderfully, and looks even better. We hope to begin dry walling this week or next. Move-in date should be mid-to-late August, before school begins we hope; during the dog days of the State Fair, I guess.

God bless you all and namaste.

Love,

Susan

Kids Educated on the Midway
Two Years Earlier

I'm ready to hit the fair for Sedalia night. I'm packing lots of cash, a map locating all of the food specials and, of course, the wine tent. But most importantly, I'm packing lots of attitude!

Last year we gave each of our daughters $15 and a wristband, and cautioned them that all of their snacks and games and souvenirs had to be purchased out of that amount. After hours of enjoying the rides, the kids were determined to try their hand at a few games, despite my admonitions that most of the games were very difficult to actually win, so I tried to guide them to the safe bets.

"Prize Every Time," the sign proclaimed as I steered my youngest daughter toward a ball toss game. When none of the balls actually landed in the basket, however, the young woman manning the booth simply said "sorry," and turned to help another customer.

"Uh, don't we get a prize?" I asked her, somewhat embarrassed at having to press the point. "The sign does advertise a prize every time," I insisted. Still, she had to check with her manager in the next booth before she could relinquish title to the tiny, plastic clacker we eventually walked away with.

Meanwhile, the rope climb had caught the eye of another daughter. She was staring, mesmerized, at a couple of teenage boys attempting to climb up rope ladders strung on an angle over an inflated, plastic pad.

"I can do that," she said, entranced. It was getting late and I was yearning to steer my gang to the exit of the midway, but I tried to keep the desperation out of my voice.

"Honey, that is a lot harder to do than it looks," I started to explain. But as if to prove me wrong, the young man in charge of the game jumped onto the first step, clambered effortlessly up the ladder, and rang the bell at the top.

"See," my daughter berated me. "It's easy!" And before I could utter another word she had stepped right up and handed the man a $5 bill.

Well, of course she fell off the ladder after two steps. But, totally determined, she immediately dusted herself off and handed him another few dollars to try again. By her third attempt, I was beside myself, knowing that she was going to waste all of her money and end up disappointed, frustrated, and without a prize.

I watched her as she slowly, meticulously steadied and balanced herself while inching up the ladder. Then, to my utter astonishment, she actually did it! After crawling slowly up the first few steps, she quickly scampered up the rest of the way, rang the bell, and promptly fell to the mat below.

"Hurray," I yelled, more excited than my daughter as I turned to find the carny, who was off talking with friends.

"Hey, she did it," I yelled excitedly when he walked over.

"Well, I didn't see it," he said, sounding incredulous that anyone other than himself could actually accomplish the task, and determined not to give an inch.

"Well just because you didn't see it, doesn't mean that she didn't win," I snapped at him, as I glanced down at my daughter's crestfallen face.

Of course, he had no idea who he was dealing with. After spending all evening on the midway, sweating through my clothes entirely, and dining on corn dogs and cotton candy, there was no way on Earth I was leaving without our prize!

We deserved that gigantic purple elephant! We had spent $9 on that thing that cost 50 cents to make in China and we were going to haul it all over the midway with us before lugging it home and throwing it in the basement so we could put it in a garage sale in three years time. Who the heck did he think he was to deny us the pleasure of that purple elephant?

"Well, I'm sorry," he was just beginning to explain, when my hero arrived. A perfect stranger marched up to us, obviously another parent, judging by the two sticky little boys he had in tow and the harried look on his sweat-stained face.

"Hey, she did it. I saw her," he emphatically exclaimed. "She ran right up there and rang that bell. You need to give her a prize."

The carny looked at the man, then back at me, and knew immediately that he had lost the battle. As we triumphantly picked out our prize, I waved to the heroic stranger who was already melting into the crowded midway.

So, if you see me arguing with a carny on the midway this year, please help me out. I figure we'll end up with better prizes if we all stick together!

Aug 22, 2007 5:46 pm

Well, it's official. I am as lethargic as my teenage daughters. I will watch whatever, anything and everything on TV, just to have an excuse to sit down for a while. Of course, I have verified what I already knew, it is all total crap.

My last MRI at the end of July showed a slight increase in my tumor. Therefore we are changing chemotherapy drugs. My nutritionist thinks I will respond well to treatment with minimal side effects. My oncologists agree. So I am ready to begin attacking the tumor again and feeling better as my symptoms subside.

Meanwhile the house is getting more beautiful every day. We're down to the fun stuff, tile, flooring, final paint colors. Hope to be moving in no later that October 1.

We continue to feel so blessed. Both of our families and many of our friends in the community continue to shower us with kindnesses and abundant blessings.

Thanks for all the prayers and support.

Love,

Susan

Summer Without Gilmore Girls and Television
Two Summers Earlier

The witty banter of the Gilmore Girls blares in my ears as I prepare dinner. As usual, my three daughters came home from school and immediately settled in front of the television, despite the glorious spring weather beckoning from the open patio door.

I can't really blame them. This is one of the few afternoons when there are no scheduled activities, and I know they need some time to rest and relax. Still, I'm eagerly looking forward to the summer months, when the television and the VCR will be shut off completely.

Yes, for the past three summers we have lived without television and the accompanying pop culture I find more and more annoying with every passing year.

Like all mothers, I was guilty when my children were much younger of planting them in front of the television so that I could get dinner ready or make a phone call without being distracted. But that carefully scheduled and structured time has morphed into almost incessant watching.

Sure, my kids are busy with lots of activities outside our house. But the minute they are bored at home, and that seems to occur the minute they walk in the door these days, they head for the television.

Invariably, if I don't insist upon turning it off, they will sit there while show after show is played. They seem to have much in common with McCaulay Caulkin's character in the "Home Alone" movies who asserts, "I'm 10, TV is my life!"

So day after day I listen, with my teeth on edge, to the too-cute repartee of the Gilmore Girls, mother and daughter and best friends to boot. They both wear a size two, are drop-dead gorgeous, and have parents/grandparents who are filthy rich. Just once I wish they'd scream at each other like any respectable real mom and teenager would do.

As irritating as Lorelei and Rory can be, however, there are lots of far worse shows out there. And even though I try to monitor what they watch, as they get older, my daughters are increasingly drawn to shows that used to be strictly verboten.

On more than one occasion I've walked into the room only to see what appears to be MTV hastily switched to the Disney Channel. Remote controls make it much harder to catch them in the act.

So, for the past two summers we turn the darn thing off completely. The first summer I had an actual panic attack the day the cable man appeared to disconnect our service. Since we live in the country, without cable, we have no television at all.

Can we really exist without television? I thought, my mind racing ahead to the long summer days filled with crabby kids. Would my kids nag and whine and complain all summer? Or rather, would they nag and whine and complain even more than they normally do all summer?

Yes, they did fight me initially, but realizing that I would not be changing my mind, they quickly resigned themselves to the dismal reality and adjusted accordingly.

The first morning, instead of plopping down in front of the television, they decided to make chocolate-chip pancakes for breakfast. An hour later the kitchen was a disaster area and they had eaten a ton of chocolate chips and very little of the actual pancakes.

What have I done? I thought ruefully as I glanced around the wreckage of the kitchen.

The next morning went much smoother. Instead of cooking, they each picked up a book and began a lazy morning of reading. Thus began a new summer habit!

In lieu of watching hours of television, zombie-like, my children began consuming every book they could get their hands on. Upon waking in the morning, they would snuggle on the couch and immediately pick up a book, even before eating breakfast or brushing their teeth.

I reinforced the habit by making countless trips to the library with them, as well as to bookstores, where they were allowed to browse as long as they liked and to purchase one or two books and then to drink hot chocolate in the café while immediately delving into their new purchase. What better way to teach that reading is a luxury and a pleasure, not a chore? And what better way to reinforce the idea that watching television is a habit like any other. Once that habit is broken, so much time opens up for more enriching experiences, like reading.

Sometimes I think my vehement objection to television has merely fueled my daughters' obsession with it during the winter months. Perhaps they watch even more during the winter because they are forced to go without for three months of the year.

But that's a trade-off I'm willing to make. And as they get older their schedules are filling up with school and sporting activities, which will further limit their viewing time during the winter months.

For now, I'll settle for quiet, peaceful summers. Sure my house is messier, and I occasionally have to play a game of Candyland or fill in as pitcher in the Wiffle ball game in the front yard. But it's well worth it, just to kick Lorelei and Rory Gilmore out of my house—for three whole months!

Sept 10, 2007 3:32 pm

My second treatment went well. I did feel some slight nausea, but after eating my way through Southern California, Manhattan and North and South Carolina this summer, it was a real relief to miss a meal. I did feel extremely fatigued and listless, but discovered it is still quite easy to shop on the couch with a catalog and cell phone.

The house is simply gorgeous. Moving date looks like October 6th.

Had a scary episode this morning over chai tea with friends as my hand was shaking uncontrollably for a bit. Thought I was having a seizure, but by the time my dear friends bundled me home, it had subsided. Another long nap!

I feel groggy but much better. Keep your prayers wending my way. They provide me great peace in my heart and soul.

The girls are great. Busy at school with friends and sports.

Love you all!

Susan

Notes for column
September 2007

I hate the fact that my first column after several months off will have to involve eating crow. But such was the topic that came unsolicited as they often do, coercing me into doing their bidding or choose to sit in frustration while the words struggle to come.

The topic whispered to me that perhaps I had been somewhat of a cry baby or whiner when my home burned down, as I waxed lyrical about how wonderful everything old is.

In reality I think I was just petrified that I would never get to be old even though my daughters think I already am at the ripe old age of 47. In any case, I still mourn my lovely old things but have also begun to appreciate the beauty and grandeur of new!

My change of heart began at the exact moment that my first new piece of furniture arrived in the living room of my summer home. The pattern of the sofa was "mini-mums" in a bright cinnabar red.

It came in via "white glove" delivery, a thing of sheer beauty: I gazed at it a full ten minutes before sinking into its plump cushions and all the connotations of new sinking into my brain—clean, pristine, nary a pizza or soda stain in sight. No holes or frayed fashion threads on the arms, no popcorn kernels or cookie crumbs embedded in the seat cushions!

Sept 29, 2007 9:05 am

My MRI went well on Thursday. At first glance both the local radiologist and oncologist called it stable, meaning no change for the better or worse!

They, of course, thought this was great given the nasty nature of GBM's. I, however, was disappointed to be doing a fairly toxic new therapy with "no change."

Even though I don't have any overt symptoms, like constant vomiting, the new drugs still kick my butt, making me feel like I'm 95, not to mention any long term effects that may develop.

While I did scarf down some peanut butter brownies from The Cake Lady this week, I have noticed that my sugar fixation has begun to wane somewhat—thank goodness!

So the next steps are three more treatments, then another MRI to be carried to Duke for a follow-up visit the week before Thanksgiving.

Meanwhile, we're set to move next week. Thursday pack, Friday load the truck, Saturday move stuff. Doty's is moving us (unbelievable, but they say that even after the house fire we still have more junk than an average household—**** it!)

My family is coming to help unload, and two sisters are staying the following week. I'm delaying my treatment by a few days with Duke's approval until after the move so I have more energy.

Love to everyone,

Susan

Thank you note
October 2007

Once again I am completely humbled and more than slightly embarrassed at having to take and take and take from the kindness and generosity of so many lovely friends and family members. And yet, I know that without all these acts of kindness, large and small, (and all the prayers) we would not have made it through these past several very stressful months!

Mary summed it up the night before school started, "We had a great summer, Mom!" she exclaimed. At first I was aghast, thinking she was teasing me.

"What?" I questioned her.

"We had a great summer," she emphatically repeated.

Did we live through the same season? I thought.

But then I rejoiced that her young intellect and spirit had filtered out the fact that Mom was tired, crabby, terrified and basically inattentive for the past five months.

Instead she only remembers long hours at the pool, countless sleepovers and numerous field trips with other families. And I am thrilled that her tenth summer will be in her memory like all the others—nearly perfect!

We are confident the new treatment will work, but continue to offer up the outcome to a higher power and to concentrate on living each day fully and creating more memories for our girls, or as William James once said, "We are willing to have it so, however 'it' turns out."

With your help it has been so much easier to concentrate on what is really important, and for that we will be eternally grateful.

God bless you.

Much love to you and yours,

Susan

Meal Deliveries an Eye-Opener
Two Years Earlier

For the past couple of weeks, I have intently followed the news from New Orleans, reading the details and viewing the pictures from the catastrophe. But after delivering Meals on Wheels last week, my mind lately has been more focused on the poor senior citizens within our own community.

Because our church was scheduled to deliver Meals on Wheels last week, I had committed myself to driving a route each day from 11 a.m. to noon, but I was not looking forward to it, thinking instead of everything I could accomplish during those precious hours spent in the car.

However, as usual, once I began my route, whatever plans I had that day paled in comparison to glimpsing the lives of our community's elderly and seeing the gratitude and loneliness written on their faces as they received each day's hot lunch.

Some of the houses are tidy and well-cared for, spick-and-span on the inside, their inhabitants obviously still able to care for themselves and their home. A bright pot of geraniums sits on one porch, offering a cheerful welcome to any who approach. Sometimes there is a relative at one of these homes, mowing the lawn, repairing a broken door hinge, replacing an inconvenient light bulb, or merely sitting and chatting. Pictures of children and grandchildren, of nieces and nephews line the top of the television, or clutter the table next to the recliner along with other crucial objects for each day: Kleenex, glass of water, medication, remote control.

"Please leave lunch on porch. I'm with my daughter," reads a note at one of the first homes on my route, and I feel a slight thrill for this sweet, frail woman who gets an outing with her daughter, perhaps just to the doctor, but out in the world, nevertheless. These are the relatively happy homes, where the pace of life, while obviously slowed, still ambles on full of small pleasures and connections to the outside world.

But there are many other kinds of homes where I deliver meals during my week of service. Many of these homes are quite the opposite. In fact, many are ramshackle, showing signs of neglect and the ravages of time, piled with years and years of accumulated debris.

At these homes, I rarely see relatives. The grass gets long and shaggy, the paint peels from the siding, the bushes grow wild and untrimmed. And the smell that emanates from the open door is, at best, musty and stale, at worst, hard to take. Perhaps it is my imagination, but the people who answer these doors always seem a little more lonely, a little more grateful to see someone on their stoop.

Often on the index card with their name and address is written, "Do Not Collect," meaning even the meager price of these delivered meals is somehow beyond them.

I turn away from these homes with a lump in my throat, wondering about these unheard and unseen members of our community. What has your life been like? I want to ask them.

Where are the people you loved and cared for during your many years here on Earth, and why are they not now here to care for you?

Then, of course, I wonder which kind of home I will end up in if I live long enough. Who will care for me if my daughters move far away, as may very well happen?

"Will you always come and visit me, even when you grow up and have a family of your own?" I ask my youngest daughter that night as I tuck her in.

"Sure," she answers instantly, "as long as you don't smell too bad."

Momentarily shocked by her reply, I realize that her after-school music club sang in several nursing homes the previous year, where she probably did meet some older people who smelled slightly. At the ripe old age of 8, she simply cannot conceive of a time when she or anyone she knows could reach such a state, when even keeping your body clean becomes an insurmountable task. The helpless elderly are as foreign and alien to her young mind as E.T.

While I desperately want to live a long life, to see my daughters grow up, and to hold my grandchildren and even great-grandchildren in my arms, I also hope that I never become one of these hidden elderly, silent, unseen, forever longing for a friendly glimpse of the world outside their door.

And even though I may grumble about it the next time I'm asked to deliver Meals on Wheels, I will do it, knowing full well that while those hot lunches are feeding some of our poor and lonely neighbors, they are nurturing my soul as well.

Nov 6, 2007 8:11 pm

Susan had an MRI in Sedalia today, the results of which she and Joe are hand carrying to Durham on Thursday so that the doctors at Duke can read them.

She'll post an update after that trip but asks everyone at this time to send her their prayers for a good result at Duke.

Kitchen Legacy One of Grace
Two Years Earlier

The very last chore my mother would perform the night before our Thanksgiving feast, was to get down on her hands and knees and scrub the kitchen floor, usually around 10:30 at night.

I used to wonder why she worked so late, when her typical routine at the end of the day was to fall asleep in the living room, with some classical tome she'd been reading collapsed upon her lap.

Once I had children of my own, however, the answer was crystal clear. Late at night was the only time the kitchen floor would have a chance to dry before our large family began to muck it up again.

The house I grew up in had been built at the turn of the century, so the kitchen was typically small and rather dark with only two small windows. The appliances were old, the wallpaper was beginning to peel in the corners, and the oven smoked like crazy when my mother baked anything at high temperatures. Some concoction was always slopping over the sides of the pan, and in the days before self-cleaning ovens, that toxic chore was never high on my working mother's list of priorities.

Still, even smoke-filled recollections of that tiny kitchen evoke such warmth in my heart. With ten children in the house, the kitchen was the center of our universe, for we were always eating or foraging for food, while my mother spent hours and hours over the sink and the stove, preparing or washing up after a meal.

The chopping and baking began bright and early on Thanksgiving morning as my mother began her holiday ritual by stuffing the turkey and baking pies.

"Why didn't you bake the pies yesterday?" I asked her one Thanksgiving Day, when I was home visiting from college, helping with preparations and basking in the presence of her vitality and creativity. She looked at me, incredulous that I could suggest such a thing. "Pies are meant to be baked the same day you eat them!" she declared.

We loved spending time with her in the kitchen, especially on holidays, when the baking and cooking became an all-day marathon. If we needed to talk with her about any important issue, there was ample time to bring it up during the hours spent preparing dinner or sipping a cup of tea at the kitchen table.

In this way, my mother imparted advice on a wide range of subjects, but her greatest strength was in her ability to listen, for she knew that if people are given a sympathetic ear, they will often arrive at their own solutions.

And while she listened, she cooked. Into her pumpkin and apple and cherry pies, her nut bread and barley casserole, her mashed sweet potatoes and sausage stuffing, she poured all of the love she felt for her family, all of the creativity of her amazing intellect and all of the expression of her artistic sensibilities. All of this she mixed and seasoned and served up to us night after night, in triple measure on Thanksgiving and Christmas and Easter, even before we were old enough to realize and appreciate the grandeur of her gift.

Today I recognize the gift for what it was, however, and I understand how it shaped and molded my character and my subsequent life choices. It was the gift of her grace, a grace that was formed and dispensed over the years in a humble, sometimes exhausting, but ever crucial way—in the kitchen.

This year I'll be hosting my own family gathering on Thanksgiving Day and cooking my own turkey dinner with all the trimmings. I may succumb to temptation and bake my pies in advance, but I'll still pull out my best damask tablecloth and use my fine china and crystal wine glasses. I'll follow her example and her ritual as much as I can, knowing that my meal will in all likelihood be far inferior to hers. But ultimately the result will be the same.

I'll be feeding the hunger in my family to be nurtured and loved, and I'll be honoring the legacy of the amazing woman who was my mother, the woman who taught me to revere the beauty in ordinary things and to take pride in doing even the most mundane of tasks with grace and gratitude.

Giving Revives Family Rivalries
Two Years Earlier

My siblings and I perform an important task every year after our Thanksgiving dinner—we pick names for our Christmas gift exchange. Simple enough, you might remark, and yet it seems to require countless conversations regarding the best way of choosing names.

Without fail, every year someone suggests that we do away with the adult name-drawing since we all have more stuff than we need or can use, and consistently buy ourselves new things throughout the year.

Furthermore, we are all in complete agreement that Christmas has gotten too hectic, too expensive and much too commercial, leaving everyone feeling rather frazzled by the season's end. Therefore, the idea of buying and wrapping a few less gifts seems like a great way to begin simplifying Christmas, especially since the gift-giving tends to get out of hand.

Even though years ago we set a $40 limit, the price tags have gradually crept upward, culminating last year with my bachelor brother modestly presenting the latest iPod to a gleeful and very appreciative nephew. Easy to do when your gift list is a mere handful of names with no obligation to fulfill a child's wish list, participate in school or church giving projects or provide teachers' presents and supplies for class parties, etc., etc., etc.

Still, despite the majority of family members feeling a little fed up with the gift exchange, there is always at least one holdout, someone who wants to continue drawing names simply because it is a tradition.

This year the conversation continued over the entire weekend after Thanksgiving, centered mainly in my sister's kitchen, while various siblings floated in and out of the house—and the conversation. At one point the names had all been written, scrunched up and many had been drawn out of a bowl before it was decided to completely revisit the process one more time.

"Well, fine!" my sister finally exclaimed, in the middle of a rather heated debate about the subject. "Just leave my name out of the drawing. And everyone who wants to be in it can put their names in."

"Uh-uh, no way," another sister quickly replied. "We're all in this together. Either we all do it, or none of us do it."

"How about if we make it a gift of meaning, a gift from the heart?" another sister suggests while the rest of us roll our eyes, fully prepared for what is coming next. "Everyone can make their gifts or wrap up something they already have."

Easy for her, I thought, since she is artistic and crafty. But the thought of making a gift that someone will actually like and use is utter torture to me, ranking right alongside making a Halloween costume or coming up with the perfect science experiment. But I rather like the idea of wrapping up something we own and passing it along to a sibling.

After all, my older brother has an extensive book collection with some very interesting titles I would love to get my hands on, and my older sister, in whose house we now sit, has a great eye when it comes to knickknacks and home furnishings. As the discussion continues I casually glance around the room wondering what gewgaw she'll wrap up if she gets my name, while at the same time wondering if I can somehow rig the drawing so she will indeed get my name. By the time I'm tuned in to the conversation again, that idea has already been discarded.

"I don't think the gift exchange should come with a long list of rules and regulations," another sister rejoins. What she really means and what so many of us still feel years and years after our childhoods have ended is, "You're not the boss of me!"

"It really would be a lot easier if we were all estranged," the sister acting as our hostess muses. And we all nod in quiet assent.

Finally, after much debate and lively discussion, we are back to the status quo. The name drawing is performed in exactly the same way it has been for years.

Luckily, I avoid drawing the name of one of my teenage nephews or nieces, since I have no idea what to buy them. I'm not sure why they're in the adult drawing anyway, but my repeated objections to this change of a few years back had met with complete resistance or worse, a complete lack of acknowledgment. ("Did somebody just say something?" I think were the exact words in response to my objections.)

"So, what are we doing now?" a niece asks as she finally draws a name from the bowl (for the third time). "Does it still need to be a gift from the heart?"

Not if you can afford an iPod, honey.

To O'Brien and Fischer families
Christmas 2007

"You people!" We sometimes sneer at each other during heated political debate.

"My people," I now think incessantly, my heart brimming over with love and appreciation.

I would rather die tomorrow having lived in the midst of such fine company than to live to be ninety among more ordinary folk!

Thanks to all of you for literally keeping me alive these two wonderful years.

With full, but peaceful hearts, we love you all dearly!

Joe, Susan, Rachel, Claire and Mary

Dec 29, 2007 5:10 pm

Susan soldiers forward although the going gets increasingly more difficult.

The whole O'Brien family went to Sedalia for Christmas Eve. I think it was good for Susan and Joe; I know it was good for the rest of us.

Jan 21, 2008
To: Family Contacts
From: Beth

I just got off the phone with Sedalia. Susan has slept three quarters of the day but did wake up and is eating a little yogurt (she had some yogurt at noon, but her appetite is waning).

She hasn't had any of her meds since last night. They weren't sure if she would be taking any this evening or not. She cannot swallow the pills now. They got a pill crusher and started using it yesterday.

Susan had a bedside chat with little Mary last night. No one is sure what was said but little Mary (Mary Margs as Susan likes to call her) stayed home from school today.

I will try to keep you posted.

Feb 10, 2008
To: Family Contacts
From: Beth

Susan has been the same for several weeks, pretty much staying in bed except for the bathroom and showering. But she eats and watches some television and talks briefly to people.

There will be a prayer service in an attempt at marshalling positive thoughts.

Feb 26, 2008 3:59 pm

The hospice nurse believes Susan is slipping into a coma and thinks the end is very close. She seems at peace.

Feb 27, 2008 12:38 pm

Susan passed away this morning at 9:26 a.m.

A prayer service will be held Sunday evening at St. Patrick's Church in Sedalia and a funeral Mass is scheduled for Monday morning.

Please send your prayers to the Fischers.

Farewell Column
March 19, 2008

Editor's note: Susan Fischer, whose first column appeared in The Sedalia Democrat in 2005, died Feb. 27, 2008. This is her last column, which she planned for publication after her death. Susan's books were lost when the Fischer house burned in February 2007. The library is a prominent feature of the home the family built after the fire.

What folly to persist in building an old-fashioned English estate-type library despite the fact that the book collection has gone up in smoke. It seems utterly ridiculous, and yet I simply can't help myself! For as long as I can remember, even as a tiny girl, I have longed for just such a room in my home. What kind of a school girl longs for a library?

I guess she must have been somewhat nerdy. She became used to getting the highest grades in the class, to not being totally surprised when the teachers suggested she skip the third grade, to staying up long after everyone else had gone to sleep just to read one more chapter, and to dominating during speech and debate class!

I can't remember the first time I picked up a book off my mother's shelf, the one that pitched me headlong into an alternate universe of prose and time so lovely that I couldn't bear to pull myself away for hours on end.

Surely it must have been Charles Dickens with his perfectly angelic heroes and heroines and his dastardly scoundrels and his always happy endings at the end of his serialized lengthy descriptions of Victorian England's society. When first I picked up the book, I only knew how beautifully and ornately it was bound and that the pictures were delightful.

Perhaps it was "Great Expectations," complete with the creepy Miss Havisham, the jilted bride, still in her wedding dress living amidst the moldering waste of her arrested life, including the remains of her wedding cake, twenty years after her fiancé stood her up at the altar.

Or maybe it was the heroism of "A Tale of Two Cities," set amidst the terror of the French Revolution. Even as a little girl, I could feel the horror of Madame Defarge, knitting, knitting—always knitting shrouds, and planning death and destruction.

Or it may have been Anna Karenina, my first glimpse into the painful, constrained existence women lived before the suffragettes battled for change.

My brilliant mother obviously had joined a book club before her marriage because she owned a dozen or so gorgeously bound classical novels which she kept in a place of honor in her bedroom. Perhaps that's why these books held instant appeal for me, rather than the juvenile books at school or the library. It never occurred to me that these books were too old for me. Drawn by the ornate binding and the pictures, I couldn't keep my hands off them. And so began a lifelong adventure galloping through literature.

After reading one selection from my mother's meager collection, I would grab other titles by the same author from the library and work my way through an entire author.

How sad I was when I finally came to the end of my local library's collection of Dickens. And how fabulous to find at the University of Missouri that the library had obscure books by Dickens I had never heard of—and so it was with all the other authors whose repertoire I thought I had already exhausted. I guess I'm a rarity, but I had actually read almost every one of the books in my collection—most of them from the classical canon.

And now I am determined to re-create the collection for my daughters. Quite probably they may not read them all like I did, or perhaps they'll turn their nose up at the old works after reading the likes of Harry Potter and "The Princess Diaries." But perhaps they'll tip headlong into each shelf and be borne along until they've read them all—and what a gift they will have received then!

"So, what books should we read, Mom?" my eldest two are already asking. Unfortunately, I'm not sure they're going to like the answer.

Start up in the corner there with Louisa May Alcott's "Little Women" and then make your way to the B's—Charlotte Bronte's "Jane Eyre," Emily Bronte's "Wuthering Heights," Anne Bronte's "Tenant of Wildfell Hall." Next, look to Willa Cather's "O Pioneers!" and to Dickens' entire collection of anthologies, novels, and short stories. Then continue on through the alphabet toward the end to Trollope's anti-heroic female characters, to Edith Wharton and her complex portrayal of characters and sad endings, and on and on. Sorry girls—there are no shortcuts through the literary canon.

Anyone who develops a love of reading, especially of the old masters, will never be bored, will have a keener insight into people and how to form healthy relationships and probably will never need therapy, since reading will give them a look into the human mind and condition. School and work will be easier; life will be easier and so much more enjoyable. They will never be bored at airports or in doctors' offices, but will carry another world in their bag with them.

Epilogue

Namasté

Eulogy

Ever since I was a little girl, the only thing I ever wanted to be was a writer. So it should come as no surprise that I would want to write my own eulogy.

Unfortunately, I did not run this by my editor, who routinely restrains me to about 700 words and since I can't find the word-count function on my new Vista operating system, I have no idea how long I'll be rambling on.

But I assume that everything I have written for today will sound smarter, funnier and more poignant, simply because I am no longer here with you. In fact, I anticipate and hope that even my daughters will be listening intently instead of rolling their eyes impatiently waiting for my latest harangue to end.

I always thought that someday I would write a great novel, something that others would read long after I was gone. I even sat down to attempt it once or twice before quickly realizing I had neither the tenacity nor the talent, the patience or the determination to bring such a project to fruition.

But as I've watched my three amazing daughters over the past two years, all of them now on the brink of becoming young women, I've come to realize that they are my masterpiece—of course, I give Joe some credit, too!

As I have wondered how you say goodbye to your children, I realized you do it the same way you embark on any spiritual journey, by first counting your blessings.

To my girls:

First Blessing

I am leaving you to the care and keeping of the best man I have ever known, your father. If you listen to your father's advice and guidance, you will have a simply marvelous life.

In fact, my girls seem to have picked up the best attributes from both of us.

I'm not sure if people truly have soul mates, but if they exist, then one definition must surely encompass the idea that soul mates bring out only what is best and true and noble in each other.

Joe has certainly done that for me and I think I have helped him on that journey as well. Sure, we've had our disagreements, but they have always been overshadowed by our mutual love, appreciation, respect and admiration for each other.

He is simply the best man I have ever known and I am completely comfortable leaving my beautiful daughters to his care and keeping.

Second Blessing

Please always remember that you come from a long line of strong, resilient women, Mary Catherine Ogier O'Brien; Maude Schnoke Karigan; Margaret Eleanor Karigan Fischer; Helen Filkohazi Ogier; Mary Louise Verlinden Fischer Norman, all of whom suffered serious adversity in their lives, but never used their struggles to escape their responsibilities or duties or to make excuses or poor choices.

I expect you girls will carry on this tradition.

I know you will be sad and grieve, but one day, joy will creep back into your heart and when it does, I want you to embrace it with all your might because even in heaven I won't be happy unless I know that you are.

In fact, I'm counting on the life force, the eternal divine source energy, to carry you through your grief.

Third Blessing

I thank God every day that you are not babies or toddlers. Instead you are all on the brink of womanhood which means I have had a hand in shaping so much of who and what you will be!

I have loved every minute of being your mother; every second and afternoon we spent on the swing set, filling the plastic wading pool, going to the library, picnicking in the park or hanging out at the swimming pool and reading, reading, reading; every second was precious to me.

And I hope those memories will sustain you and guide you when you have your own children.

Ultimately, we have had so many great years together that really you know all about me and how I would respond to a situation, and how I would hope that you would respond.

Fourth Blessing

I am thrilled that you will continue your life in this wonderful community of Sedalia, where all these people around you today will take care of you and know your history, your parents and grandparents.

They will hold you to a higher moral code, higher expectations than just what feels easy and good.

Everywhere you go you will always be my daughters, and I know you will continue to make me proud in that regard.

Fifth Blessing

You have so many amazing women role models in your life: aunts, older cousins, my friends, Grandma. Call on these women, both young and old, when you need them. They will love and sustain you.

I am confident that we will see each other again and that when you pray and meditate, we will communicate in the silence.

I love you dearly,
Mom

Acknowledgements

This labor of love would not have been possible without the combined efforts of the Fischer and O'Brien families, especially the talents and expertise of Ellen Heitman Walz and Annie Cosby, whose layout, design and editing beautifully reflect the magic and wonder of Susan's spirit.

About Susan O'Brien Fischer

Susan O'Brien Fischer was a journalist, wife and mother who left behind a record of her thoughts and feelings about the difficult last few years of her life—a life cut unnaturally short.

She was the seventh child in a family of ten raised in Ferguson, MO, a tree-filled suburb of St. Louis. She earned a bachelor's degree in journalism from the University of Missouri School of Journalism, as well as a minor in German. She later earned a master's degree in English Literature from Central Missouri State University.

She married her college sweetheart, Joe Fischer, after dating for ten years.

During her life, she traveled extensively in Europe on a shoestring budget; wrote news articles for a St. Louis weekly newspaper; wrote a travel column in California; owned two restaurants at the Lake of the Ozarks in Missouri; taught university writing classes and wrote a column for *The Sedalia Democrat* in the small Missouri town where she finally settled down with Joe.

But her passion and life's work—first and foremost—was making a home for her family; raising, supporting and loving her girls and sharing it all with the love of her life in a fairy-tale romance come true.